# The National Game

# THE
# NATIONAL
# GAME

*Baseball and American Culture*

## JOHN P. ROSSI

*Chicago* • *Ivan R. Dee* • *2000*

Photography credits: AP/Wide World, pages 168, 190; Brown Brothers, pages 2, 50, 74, 146, 210; Culver Pictures, pages 24, 96, 120.

Library of Congress Cataloging-in-Publication Data:
Rossi, John P.
    The national game : baseball and American culture / John P. Rossi.
      p.  cm.
    Includes bibliographical references and index.
    ISBN 1-56663-287-0 (alk. paper)
    1. Baseball—Social aspects—United States—History.  I. Title.
GV867.64.R68  2000
796.357'0973—dc21                                                                99-053674

*For my brothers,*
*Angelo (1937–1999), Raymond, and Vincent*

# Preface

FIFTY YEARS AGO, at my new local library, I asked the formidable-looking head librarian if she had any books on the history of baseball. She glared at me through her gold pince-nez: "I know of none," was her sharp retort. "You should be reading something more worthwhile."

Madam Librarian was right: in the early 1950s there was virtually nothing of value in serious baseball history. What existed was either journalistic or of poor quality and reliability. But she was also very wrong: baseball's past has proven to be a rich subject for study.

Over the last half-century this dearth of solid baseball research has been overcome. Partly this has resulted from the fact that no other sport so deeply touches the American psyche. Beginning with Harold Seymour's groundbreaking monograph *Baseball: The Early Years*, published in 1960, the study of baseball and its relation to American history has become a growth industry. Seymour demonstrated that a first-rate historian could explore the past of America's game without wallowing in myth. His book, and its succeeding volume, *The Golden Years*, were nothing less than the foundation on which all later historical research into baseball was built.

Following Seymour's work, David Voigt, in his three-volume study called, simply enough, *American Baseball,* traced the links between the game and key developments in American history. The title of one of his shorter studies, *America Through Baseball,* aptly summarizes Voigt's approach.

Since the early 1960s serious historical studies have investigated just about every corner of America's connection to baseball. Scholars such as Steven Riess have considered the question of baseball and social mobility as well as the sport's relationship to ethnicity. Benjamin Rader has written the most recent short but solid overview of baseball as well as one of the best studies of the role of sport in American history, *American Sports: From the Age of Folk Games to the Age of Televised Sports.* Historians such as Melvin Adelman, Stephen Freedman, and Warren Goldstein have unearthed enormous detail about the early history of baseball in America.

At the same time traditional histories of baseball teams and biographies of the great players have poured forth. Robert Creamer's studies of Babe Ruth and Casey Stengel, Charles Alexander's life of Ty Cobb, and Jules Tygiel's study of Jackie Robinson are models of this approach.

Serious quarterlies such as the *Journal of Sport History* and *The International Journal of the History of Sport,* published in England, have presented scholarly work on unusual aspects of baseball's past. Amateur enthusiasts have made their contribution too. The Society of American Baseball Research, in two fine publications, *The National Pastime* and the *Baseball Research Journal,* has done important work in probing various aspects of the game's history.

As a result, it has been possible to look at baseball and its history in much the same way as we do the history of a corporation, a religious denomination, or an ethnic group. Baseball is no longer regarded as an invalid field of study. Yogi Berra once noted that "you can observe a lot by watching." You also can learn a lot of American history through baseball.

The purpose of my book is to provide an overview of the connections between professional baseball and America's history over the past 175 years. My hope is that it will provide a way for those interested in America's past to approach its rich history in a different yet rewarding way. I have concentrated on the role of major league baseball since its formulation in the last quarter of the nineteenth century. The history of the minor leagues and amateur baseball constitute, in my view, a separate and interesting chapter in baseball's history.

Many people helped in this work. My wife Frances and daughter Monica provided needed support at home. The Research Leave Committee of La Salle University granted me a reduced schedule to work on this project. I thank them. And I want to express my appreciation for the excellent librarians at the Connelly Library of La Salle, Eithne Bearden and Stephen Breedlove, who helped me find countless source materials.

J. P. R.

*Jenkintown, Pennsylvania*
*October 1999*

# Contents

| | Preface | vii |
|---|---|---|
| 1 | Origins of the Game | 3 |
| 2 | Baseball as Big Business, 1876–1891 | 25 |
| 3 | Coming of Age, 1891–1908 | 51 |
| 4 | The Wars of Baseball, 1909–1918 | 75 |
| 5 | Golden Age, 1919–1931 | 97 |
| 6 | Baseball in Depression and War, 1931–1945 | 121 |
| 7 | No Golden Age: Baseball, 1946–1960 | 147 |
| 8 | Coming Apart, 1961–1977 | 169 |
| 9 | Best of Times, Worst of Times, 1978–1994 | 191 |
| 10 | The Future of the National Game | 211 |
| | Notes | 219 |
| | A Note on Sources | 227 |
| | Index | 236 |

# The National Game

*The Boston championship team of 1874.*

# Chapter 1

# ORIGINS
# OF THE GAME

BASEBALL HAS FORMED an intimate link with American history and culture for more than a century and a half. No other sport has imbedded itself so deeply in the national psyche or has generated such a large body of serious literature, from Ring Lardner's "You Know Me Al" stories right through Bernard Malamud's *The Natural* and Mark Harris's *Bang the Drum Slowly*. At the level of popular culture, "Casey at the Bat" and "Take Me Out to the Ball-Game" are among the most recognizable of sports motifs. Our everyday language abounds with baseball terminology: out in left field, cleanup hitter, strike out, grand slam.

Unlike the other American games of football or basketball, baseball has taken on mythic qualities. Its supposed invention by Abner Doubleday, one day in the summer of 1839, has been honored by the American government with a postage stamp. Although research has undermined the Doubleday myth, its persistence tells us much about the hold that baseball has on the American consciousness. The public has believed the Doubleday story for so long because it appeals to the American sense of uniqueness. Americans want the sport that as early as 1856 was called the national pastime to have sprung into existence like some immaculate conception, owing nothing to any other game or especially to any other nation.

In fact baseball emerged in the early nineteenth century as a unique game in America—at a particular time and particular place—for a variety of reasons. The game was not the result of a single invention or spontaneous eruption; it evolved over the years from various bat-and-ball games played in England and the American colonies. The two strongest influences creating the new game of baseball were the old English game of rounders and offshoots of it such as "town ball" and "old cat." In these games, where the number of players could vary, a ball was hit by a batter swinging a stick, who then proceeded to run from one base to another (the number of bases also varied). The rules for rounders were more formalized; the "old cat" and "town ball" games changed depending on the number of players and even whether the game was played on a city lot or in more open country. There is ample evidence of these games being played and even the name *base ball* being used in the eighteenth and early nineteenth centuries. For example, George Ewing, a soldier in George Washington's army at Valley Forge, in April 1778 recorded in his journal playing a game "base." Many illustrations can be found of men and boys playing a recognizable form of baseball in books and pamphlets published in the early nineteenth century.

Baseball began to take on its modern formulation in the 1840s, especially in the northeastern corner of the United States where the English sporting tradition was strongest. The country was changing rapidly as a result of cheap transportation and the spread of education. Cities were experiencing a huge expansion. In the 1840s, while the population of the nation grew by 36 percent, that of cities and towns of over eight thousand increased by 90 percent. In these sprawling cities baseball took hold as the public sought an outlet for its energies and a way to spend its leisure time.

The new nation had no organized sports, though cricket, horse racing, and hunting were popular. Middle-class shop-keepers, clerks, small manufacturers, and skilled craftsmen in the growing cities wanted a more organized outlet for their energies. They also sought to emulate the club tradition of England where cricket had emerged seventy years earlier. Cricket remained popular in the United States up to the 1860s. It was played mainly by the wealthy, though America continued the English tradition of working-class cricket clubs.

Baseball's growth coincided with the expansion of cricket, but in the 1860s the new game finally pulled away form its English cousin. American writers observed that baseball was "the equal of cricket as a scientific game"—that is, as a game requiring the mental powers of judgment, calculation, and quick perception. More important, as the *American Chronicle of Sports and Pastimes* boasted in 1868, baseball had changed more in ten years than cricket had in four hundred, and in doing so had adapted to its American circumstances.

The newly rich middle classes in America shared the English enthusiasm for sport and the value of outdoor exercise as a way of overcoming the dangers of a sedentary life, which was believed to promote bad habits. It was among these men that baseball first emerged. The social aspect of the game was a powerful attraction. Clubs and fraternal organizations of all kinds sprung up in the second quarter of the nineteenth century throughout the United States, helping to build America's reputation as a nation of inveterate joiners with their volunteer fire companies and numerous fraternal and religious societies.

We will never know the exact process by which baseball

developed, but it is clear that by the 1840s the game in some form was being played enthusiastically, especially in the area from Pennsylvania north through New York and into New England. It developed differently from place to place, but the level of play became more sophisticated and forms of the game enormously popular. Baseball clubs appeared in almost every town and city of any consequence. At first the game was played mostly by the better-off younger members of the middle class. (Workingmen who had to work longer hours did not have the opportunity to take off in the late afternoon for exercise, nor did they have the money to pay club dues or the costs of equipment or uniforms.) Yet the game was broadly popular, even among working-class young men who took every opportunity to play baseball. Within a few years, by one estimate, two-thirds of the early baseball players came from a working-class background while the remaining third was of the artisan class.

One of the most appealing aspects of the new game for the working classes was the simplicity of the equipment required—just a bat and a ball, and a space to play in. Any open field or city lot would suffice. The simplicity of the game was one of the reasons for its rapid spread. Cricket's influence was evident in the social aspect of early baseball. Often the games were followed by a dinner held in a tent on the playing grounds, or the players and their guests might retire to a nearby pub to celebrate. At first, victory or defeat was not as important as the excuse for a social gathering. But that soon changed.

Among the most popular forms of baseball was the Philadelphia version, in which home base was an iron plate while the playing field was diamond-shaped and the batter was retired if he was tagged out or the ball was thrown to the base ahead of him. In the Massachusetts game the field was rectangular, with ten to fourteen players on defense while bases or bounds, usually sticks, were located sixty feet apart at each corner of the field. These games clearly blended rounders with elements of town ball. Then, in 1845, Alexander Cartwright, a bank teller and volunteer fireman in New York, codified a set of rules for his baseball club, the Knickerbockers. This was a club of gentlemen, prosperous businessmen and merchants who desired vigorous athletic activity which baseball provided. They were also "men who were at liberty after 3 o'clock in the afternoon," unlike laborers who would have no time during the week for recreation.

Cartwright's scheme borrowed the diamond shape from the Philadelphia game, placed the pitcher or bowler forty-five feet from the batter, and set the bases ninety feet apart. The bases were canvas bags, not sticks or stones, while home plate and the pitcher's plate were round iron disks. Cartwright specified nine players, distributing them essentially as they are today except for the shortstop, who moved about the infield. As in the other versions of baseball, the pitcher's job was to put the ball in play, not to get the batter out. He threw softly underhand. The batter was out if the ball was caught in the air or on one bounce, or if the fielder threw the ball to the base before the runner arrived there. In other forms of baseball the batter was "soaked" or hit by the ball (thrown by a fielder) and put out. Cartwright ended the inning when three outs were made; the game was over when one side scored twenty-one runs, or "aces."

Cartwright's invention, soon known as the "New York game," was fast with plenty of hitting and fielding action. It was livelier than the more leisurely cricket and could be played on any field because it didn't require manicured grounds.

The popularity of the New York game grew and spread

throughout the North and East, reflecting the growing power of New York City itself as the nation's leading metropolitan area. By 1850 New York's population was 516,000, or 176,000 more than the second-largest city, Philadelphia. New York was also at the center of a main railroad hub and enjoyed the largest port traffic in the nation. Thus it was perfectly suited to spread Cartwright's new game. But in the final analysis the success of the New York game was rooted in its logic and simplicity: it was easy to learn and relatively easy to master. Cartwright's rules were in such demand that he had more than 100 copies printed. An address placed in the *Sunday Mercury* indicated where baseball clubs could write for further information about his innovations.

By 1860, with the addition of a few refinements, such as the adoption of the nine-inning concept from the Philadelphia game and the requirement that fly balls be caught in the air rather than on one bounce, Cartwright's version became the most popular form of baseball being played. Other forms of baseball as well as cricket continued to be played for some years, but they too gave way to the New York game. By the onset of the Civil War, American newspapers were carrying detailed, inning-by-inning scores of games. The rise of the cheap penny press led to increased sports coverage, helping baseball gain a new audience. The weekly *New York Clipper,* founded in 1853, and the *Police Gazette* (1845) devoted considerable space to baseball. *Beadle's Dime Base-Ball Player* first appeared in 1860 and sold between fifty thousand and sixty thousand copies annually. Perhaps most important, the game benefited from its affinity for statistics, still one of baseball's greatest strengths when measured against other popular sports.

At first, writers counted runs as in cricket. But Henry Chadwick, an English immigrant and one of the first sportswriters, around 1860 invented the method for compiling batting averages as well as the first "box score." Chadwick's idea was to provide a clear statistical breakdown of the game by showing the number of runs, hits, and outs recorded by each player. The box score, which might have been inspired by cricket scoring, caught on quickly because it was a simple way of showing what had happened in a particular game. Together with the idea of batting averages, box scores launched the statistical life of baseball whereby players and teams may be compared in a way denied other sports. A glance at any sports page today shows the continuing popularity of baseball statistics. Baseball is the only sport, in fact, where statistics reveal anything important about the game. The best hitter has the highest batting average; the most powerful, the most home runs. Pitchers can be measured by wins, percentage of victories, earned runs allowed per nine innings, or games saved. Almost from the beginning, the new sport of baseball was a mathematical wonder.

Chadwick ranks with Albert Goodwill Spalding as one of the key figures in spreading the popularity of baseball. He reported the game for various newspapers in the New York area and edited the first true baseball guides: *Beadle's Dime Base-Ball Player* and *Spalding's Official Base Ball Guide.* In 1868 Chadwick also wrote the first serious analysis of the sport: *The Game of Base Ball: How to Learn It, How to Play It, and How to Teach It.* In many ways, as much as any individual he deserves the title the "Father of Baseball." He not only wrote enthusiastically and expertly about the sport, he literally preached the gospel of baseball. After seeing his first game he noted, "I was struck with the idea that base ball was just the game for a national sport for Americans, and . . . I came to the conclusion that from this game of ball . . . our people could be lifted into a position of more devotion to physical exercise and healthful outdoor recreation." From this view Chadwick never deviated.

A clear sign of baseball's popularity occurred on the eve of the Civil War. In 1860 the Excelsior Club of Brooklyn undertook the first tour of a baseball nine, traveling by train throughout New York State and then down to Pennsylvania, Maryland, and Delaware, playing before large crowds that were already deeply informed about baseball. The success of this tour showed the possibility of spreading the game throughout the nation now that a railway network was near completion. Journeys that would have seemed impossible in the 1840s now were commonplace. It can be argued that baseball's acceptance as America's game paralleled the spread of the railroad to every corner of the pioneering nation. By the 1880s baseball was known or played throughout the country, just when the railway network bound the nation together.

The enthusiastic adoption of baseball fit the national mood. The game gave the country a sport that was not quite cricket, not quite rounders, and perfectly suited to the contours of the country—it was fast, dynamic, and uniquely American. America was changing with incredible speed. Railroad mileage tripled in the 1840s. Steamboats on the Mississippi linked the Midwest with the South, with the 1,440-mile trip from New Orleans to Louisville taking just four days in 1853. The 1840s saw the largest influx of immigrants to that time in American history. More than a million Irish and a million Germans entered the country in the years 1846–1855, bringing with them new attitudes, tastes, and standards. They were searching for ways to identify themselves with their new home. Baseball was one such way.

Baseball's appeal initially was to an older generation of Americans and was largely nostalgic. Because most men had played some form of it as children, they could identify with baseball and enjoy playing or watching. It gave the businessmen in cities and towns a way to relive their youth. One of them, Frank Pigeon of the Brooklyn Eckford Club, summed up this aspect of the new game. He saw baseball as a way for he and his friends to "forget business and everything else, go out on the green fields, don our ball suits, and go at it with a rush. At such times we were boys again." Sport in general and baseball in particular was important for the newly powerful middle classes because it was believed to relieve anxieties, discourage impulsive behavior, and teach important qualities such as leadership and cooperation. Although conceived originally as an outlet for the middle class, baseball was also seen as a way of socializing the energies of the more impetuous lower classes. It would lose its amateur qualities within a single generation.

By the outbreak of the Civil War there were hundreds of baseball clubs of all kinds in America, and baseball was rapidly on its way to becoming the national game. Four years after the war ended, the *New York Herald* estimated that the number of active baseball clubs had climbed to over a thousand. The sport had moved from an informal game to a fraternal one in less than a generation. It was being played with greater professionalism and sophistication, and in the process was undergoing subtle changes. In 1863 it was decided that fly balls had to be caught in the air and not on one bounce in order to be out. In 1867 catchers, who originally stood fifty feet behind the batter, now moved closer to home plate. A few years later Fred Thayer of Harvard made an iron bird-cage mask to protect the catcher's face, adapting the idea from fencing. The fraternal element generated intense competition and rivalries both within cities and between cities. Large crowds began to turn out for important games.

Baseball after the Civil War, like the nation, was ready to take off.


## *The Professional Game*

ACCORDING TO most authorities, the Civil War hindered the development of baseball as the nation dealt with more important business. We know that baseball was played during the Civil War as there is a painting of Union prisoners of war playing the game in Salisbury, North Carolina, in 1862. Some evidence shows that a baseball game was played around Christmastime in New York that same year between a team from the 165th New York Infantry and an all-star squad. Reports give the crowd as forty thousand, which is certainly too high for the time. Also in 1862 a team of Philadelphia players invaded Gotham to play a series of games against New York, Brooklyn, and Newark. These contests helped revive baseball in the midst of the war.

Various forms of baseball were played in the South, although not as extensively as in the North. The war introduced the game to more men both North and South, who brought it back to their communities outside the Northeast where baseball first took root. The war certainly created a desire to find unifying themes for a desperately divided nation. Baseball helped fill that desire. Already called the National Game before the war, baseball provided a ritual and sport around which the country could rally. The years after the Civil War saw an explosion of interest in the game. As the *Newark Daily Advertiser* noted, the end of the war brought a virtual baseball boom throughout the nation. Some baseball supporters hoped it could help heal the wounds caused by the war. Northern teams that traveled south to play were not always greeted warmly, but gradually the Southern cities and towns began to embrace the new game. *Wilke's Spirit,* a New York paper, noted that the New York Mutual team had been received warmly in New Orleans on an exhibition tour. "This National Game," it observed hopefully, "seems destined to close the National Wounds opened by the late war. It is no idle pastime which draws young men, separated by two thousand miles, together to contest in friendship, upon fields but lately crimsoned with their brothers' blood in mortal combat."

Baseball's new popularity was reflected in many different ways after the Civil War. Popular songs and dances drew on baseball themes, such as "The Live Oak Polka" and "The Baseball Polka." A child's board game invented in the 1860s was called "Baseball." We also know that colleges had integrated baseball into their sports programs as early as the late 1850s. In fact, convincing evidence shows that baseball was the most popular college sport in the last half of the nineteenth century. The first intercollegiate game was played on July 1, 1859, between Amherst and Williams College. Amherst won by a typical early baseball score of 73 to 32. A wonderful series of evocative photos, recently discovered, shows a recognizable game of baseball at Wesleyan College around 1867. The players are clearly at their regular positions, and the pitcher is about to deliver the ball with an underhand or submarine motion. Fans dressed in top hats are scattered around the edges of the field.

Some evidence indicates that President Lincoln and his son Tad attended a baseball game in Washington during the Civil War. Connecting the martyred president to baseball was typical of the way the first generation of its supporters sought to give the game a national identity. Bill Stern, the popular (and overly imaginative) radio broadcaster of the 1930s and 1940s used to tell a dramatic tale of the assassination of Lincoln. With his last breath the dying president reached out from his deathbed to the officer sitting beside him: "Don't let them destroy baseball," he said. Then, after a pause, Stern would say, "That officer was none other than Abner Doubleday, the inventor of baseball." Of course, Lincoln never regained consciousness after he was shot, and Doubleday was nowhere near Washington that night. But myth is sometimes stronger than reality. Baseball by the 1860s had arrived as an American phenomenon.

In 1858 a group of amateur baseball clubs met in New York to organize a ruling body, the National Association of Base Ball Players. This group assumed the responsibility for rule making and for maintaining the fraternal nature of the game. It also sought to promote the new sport and, in proper Victorian form, to maintain its integrity. By the end of the war the Association represented 91 clubs drawn from 10 states. Three years later that number had jumped to 350 clubs as baseball took its position as the leading sport in America, a position it held for a century.

The success of the NABBP reflected baseball's astounding growth: the game had spread to every corner of the country, including California. But growth also brought problems. Competition created a need to win. To find the best players, clubs began to lose their amateur flavor as they brought in paid players who were enlisted not for fraternal reasons but to produce victories. Baseball entered what Harold Seymour called the twilight zone between amateurism and professionalism. It was only a matter of time before professionalism took hold, because it was becoming clear by the 1860s that there was money to be made on baseball. By charging admission—even if only ten cents—teams could turn a profit.

The intense competition generated by baseball in the

years after the Civil War also promoted another dimension of the sport that was deeply rooted in American history— gambling. Americans had inherited from their English fore- bears a love of gambling, and nothing lent itself better to that activity than betting on a team or an individual. With its evil twin, alcoholism, gambling would plague baseball throughout its history and at times threaten the very existence of the game.

The National Association of Base Ball Players dissolved in the late 1860s, plagued by schedule breakdowns, poorly or- ganized teams, and players jumping from one team to an- other—called "revolving" in those days. The Association also suffered from the domination of the New York Knickerbocker Club that acted as if it owned the new sport.

In 1869 the first truly professional team, the Cincinnati Red Stockings, was formed. The Cincinnati team had been a member of the amateur Association, but team owners wanted to build a successful winning team. They turned to profes- sionals and hired Harry Wright, star outfielder for the Union cricket team, for an annual salary of $1,200 and gave him carte blanche to form a winning club. Wright signed his brother, George, a talented professional cricket player for the highly regarded Philadelphia Cricket Club, at a salary of $1,400. Other professionals were hired, with the lowest-paid player receiving $600. The entire payroll came to $9,300, a considerable sum in those days. These salaries compare favor- ably with a substantial middle-class income, which in the 1870s averaged approximately $1,000; a common laborer might make about $350 and a miner $450 a year. Thus base- ball already offered an income that made it attractive to any male with athletic skill. Money not only changed the game into a professional sport, it also helped destroy its gentle- manly aspect. Young men honed their baseball skills no matter what social class they came from, because baseball paid better than most occupations.

Historians argue over the question of how deeply baseball affected social mobility in America, but there is little doubt that many young men used it to climb to financial success as well as achieve fame. The players who made up the Red Stockings listed occupations—jeweler, clerk, hatter, bookkeeper—that indicated working-class or lower-middle-class status. Professional baseball gave these men an opportunity to earn incomes far beyond those of their peers. Baseball was becoming a form of male identity and a status symbol for those who could play the game.

Long before George Steinbrenner, the 1869 Cincinnati club showed what money could do for a baseball team. Harry Wright put the team through a rigorous training program which honed its skills beyond those of other amateur and semi-professional clubs. In 1869 the Red Stockings played 58 games, including 6 against all-star squads, winning 57 and tying 1, a record sure to remain unbroken. They overpowered their opponents by such scores as 103 to 8 and 65 to 1. Low-scoring games were rare in those days of slow pitching and numerous errors. The Red Stockings, it is estimated, played before 200,000 people that season, the year the transcontinental railroad was completed, and traveled more than 12,000 miles and as far as California. President Grant arranged a meeting with the players when they were in Washington and congratulated them on their success. If politicians wished to be associated with the game, it was a sure sign that baseball had arrived.

The Red Stockings won 27 straight games to open the 1870 season. They did not lose their first game until June, when the Brooklyn Atlantics defeated them in a dramatic 11-inning game, 8 to 7, before a crowd estimated by *Harper's*

*Weekly* at 10,000 to 15,000 people who paid 50 cents each to see the game. With gate receipts of $5,000 to $7,500 for this one game, baseball was now clearly a financial success.

The Red Stockings also made a sartorial contribution to the new sport of baseball. The team introduced the knee britches or knicker type of uniform that soon caught on with other baseball clubs, replacing the long pants previously worn by ballplayers. A glance at photographs of Red Stockings players shows that the basic baseball uniform has changed surprisingly little since the 1870s. The players then wore cleated high-top shoes, garrison-style caps with a short bill to shade their eyes, and short collars usually turned up. The Red Stockings also wore a letter C on their chest to identify the team. With few modifications, this type of costume still prevails. The continuity of the uniform is one reason for baseball's popularity. Of all sports, the elements of baseball change most gradually, making it easy for its fans to connect with its past.

In the late 1860s and early 1870s the game itself continued to evolve. At the time it resembled the modern game of fast-pitch softball more than baseball. By the 1870s the baseball began to take on the look of the modern ball, shrinking to its present size of 9 to 9¼ inches in circumference and 5 to 5½ ounces in weight from the softer, larger ball used earlier in the century. The 1870s baseball consisted of a small core of hard rubber, surrounded with tightly wrapped wool and covered with two carefully stitched figure-eight pieces of horsehide, which gave the ball its distinctive look. Earlier baseballs had been stitched with a cover that looked like a peeled orange.

By the early 1870s the pitcher, still using an underhand motion, began to throw harder, trying to deceive the hitter rather than allowing him to put the ball in play. Asa Brainerd of the Red Stockings was famous for his fast pitch that he delivered with a last-second snap of the wrist. Harry Wright developed a "dew drop," or what we would now call a change of pace, to throw hitters off balance. The batter might still wait for a pitch he liked, but it soon became common for the umpire to call strikes if the batter stalled. In one famous case, a hitter for the New York Mutuals took fifty pitches before swinging. Giving the umpire the right to call strikes speeded up the game.

Batters also began to adjust their swing and stance to avoid hitting soft fly balls that were now easy outs, as outfielders rarely muffed them. Instead the batter tried to hit line drives or hard grounders, called "daisy cutters," which had a better chance of being hits. Only the pitcher and catcher wore gloves by the early 1870s, but they were little more than leather gloves with the fingers cut out. The rest of the fielders played bare-handed, thus the large number of errors and hard-hit balls that went untouched. Still, by this time the quality of play was quite high on a professional club. By the early 1870s it was rare for a professional team to lose to an amateur club, as had often happened in the past. In 1871 the Boston Red Stockings played thirty-two games against amateur competition and won every game.

Professionalism had arrived. A period of amalgamation and consolidation typical of business throughout the country in the last quarter of the nineteenth century now characterized the National Game. Professional baseball at the major-league level was about to become a monopoly or a trust.

## *The First Major League*

AFTER THE 1870 season some of the owners and managers of the teams in the National Association of Base Ball Players became dissatisfied with the league's performance. They saw the potential of making a tidy profit out of the new game. In March 1871 team owners from ten NABBP cities met in New York to form a new league, the National Association of Professional Base Ball Players. The new key word was "professional," for the ball players themselves ran the league. Consequently the league suffered from the kind of chaos one would expect when the inmates run the asylum: sloppy scheduling, poor management, incompetent business practices and constant "revolving," a plethora of gambling scandals, and, with the emergence of professionalism, a number of unsavory players. Despite these problems the new league survived for a few years until a combination of mistakes destroyed it.

The new league established teams in nine cities, four of which were in the Midwest: the Chicago White Stockings, Cleveland Forest Citys, Fort Wayne Kekiongas, and Rockford Forest Citys. The other five teams were located in the heart of what had always been baseball country, the urban areas of the Northeast: the Boston Red Stockings, New York Mutuals, Philadelphia Athletics, Washington Olympics, Washington Nationals, and Troy (New York) Haymakers. League rules were simple (but were not, as it turned out, always adhered to). It took just ten dollars to join the Association, and each club agreed to play a five-game series against every other club and to make two trips to the other cities in the league. A league championship was to be awarded the team with the best record.

Matters got off to a bad start when Fort Wayne dropped out in mid-season 1871, to be replaced by the Brooklyn Eckfords, who themselves lasted only a year. The Chicago White Stockings, who boasted a new ballpark, had to leave the city when the Great Fire of 1871 burned them out of their home.

Despite all the positive improvements over the first baseball association, the new league also suffered from birth pangs.

Probably its most serious problem was instability. Teams were founded and folded with incredible rapidity: twenty-four different teams played in the new league in just five seasons. Only three teams—the Boston Red Stockings, who were made up of defectors from Cincinnati, the New York Mutuals, and the Philadelphia Athletics—played through the entire history of the league. Some clubs lasted just one season, some even less. While the quality of play was high and fan interest surged in such cities as New York, Chicago, and Boston, where the Red Stockings drew seventy thousand fans in 1875, the overall performance of the new league was disastrous. Gambling scandals were common, and newspapers carried stories of players throwing games and gamblers giving odds and taking bets at games. The reputation of the New York Mutuals did not improve when it was discovered that William Marcy Tweed, the corrupt boss of Tammany Hall, owned part of the team.

Whiskey was sold at games in New York, leading to rowdy fan behavior, with fans spilling onto the field and interfering with games, and umpire baiting, which had been rare in baseball. Henry Chadwick, always the voice of respectable baseball, was aghast at crooked players and fixed games and campaigned for a return to the gentlemanly level of an earlier era.

Players in the new league were true professionals. Double plays became commonplace while hitting and pitching clearly exceeded the amateur level of play. In 1872 an outfielder, Jim Hatfield, threw a baseball 400 feet, 7½ inches, a feat not matched for 70 years. The number of runs scored declined during the five years of the league from 13 per game for the best team to 10.5, a sign that a balance was being achieved be-

tween offense and defense. The 100-to-10 scores of the past
were becoming rare.

The overwhelming majority of players came from urban
areas in the east. Philadelphia produced forty, New York
twenty-two, and Brooklyn thirty-six players on the league's
roster. Seven players were born in England and five in Ireland,
the latter foreshadowing the first wave of Irish American players who would come to dominate the game in the next three
decades. As early as 1871 an Irish-born player, Tony Foley of
County Cashel, briefly managed the Chicago club. Foley was a
forerunner of the McGraws, Macks, and Hanlons who would
dominate baseball managing by the 1890s. Thus for the first
time the Yankee character of baseball was being challenged.
The South and West were virtually unrepresented on the rosters of the league teams.

Play in the new league was dominated by the Boston Red
Stockings. Harry Wright had brought with him to Boston the
best of the old Cincinnati team, and he added new talent, such
as Albert G. Spalding, a great athlete who was to be one of the
key figures in the development of baseball in the last third of
the nineteenth century. Boston finished third in 1871 behind
Chicago and Philadelphia and then won the championship
easily for the next four seasons. At first the championship season encompassed just thirty games, but by 1875 the teams
were playing eighty-game seasons.

In 1874, in an attempt to make a financial killing, Wright
and Spalding hit upon the idea of touring England and showing off the new American game. The tour interrupted the regular season and showed how greatly financial considerations
now controlled baseball. Wright and Spalding were motivated
by two contrary but linked ideas—nationalism and the desire
to make money. Two talented teams, the Red Stockings and
Philadelphia Athletics, spent more than six weeks touring

England, giving demonstrations of baseball to indifferent and confused Englishmen. Spalding had also arranged for the Americans to play cricket matches which the Americans won handily, astonishing the English with their hitting and fielding prowess. What the American players did wasn't "quite cricket"—whaling away at pitches and driving the ball incredible distances compared to the more scientific strategy of cricket play favored by the English—but it was successful. The Americans won all their cricket matches but one. Wright worried that the American brand of play would alienate the English by its ungentlemanly roughness, especially as he was concerned to show them that America had developed a game worth imitating.

The British were impressed by the speed and action of baseball but showed little interest in emulating the Americans. The tour proved to be a financial disaster, costing the Americans more than $3,000 and forcing the players to take a pay cut. The Wright-Spalding tour was the first of a series over the years where baseball people thought the mere exposure of the new American sport to the rest of the world would lead to its adoption—and to even greater profits for them. Innocence combined with avarice overrode common sense. Except for peculiar adoptions in places as different as Japan and parts of the Caribbean, baseball remained a uniquely American game.

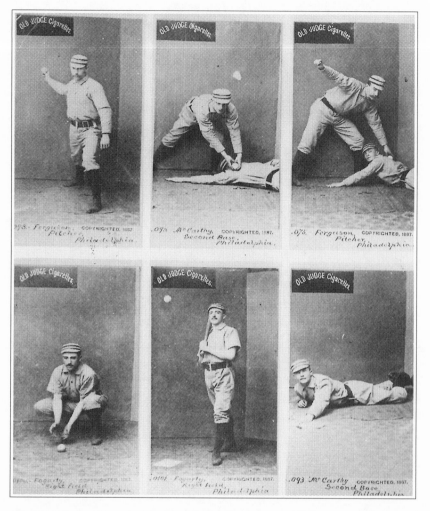

*Early baseball cards from 1887, featuring Philadelphia players.*

# Chapter 2

# BASEBALL AS
# BIG BUSINESS,
# 1876–1891

BY THE MID-1870s baseball had established itself in the ethos of American society. With few rivals as a spectator sport, the game was played throughout the nation, though its roots were deepest in the Northeast and old Midwest. Accepted by the public as uniquely American and democratic, it was a sport that all could enjoy and that the most talented, no matter their social class or background, could play. The penny press promoted baseball avidly as it sought to reach the lower classes, now growing more literate. Sports coverage facilitated by the spread of the telegraph could be found in most newspapers by the 1880s, some of it shamelessly promoting the game. Joseph Pulitzer, for example, devoted an entire section of the *St. Louis Post-Dispatch* to sports news that was largely baseball. Other newspapers followed suit.

Serious thinkers were paying attention to baseball for the first time. Some found it a disgusting spectacle with its rowdy, alcoholic, cigar-smoking fans; others thought it captured the essence of Americanism. Mark Twain, no romantic, once described baseball as "the very symbol, the outward and visible expression of all the drive and push and struggle of the raging, tearing, booming nineteenth century."

The emergence of full-fledged professional major leagues in the late 1870s and early 1880s reflected that "raging" and "tearing" character of the sport. Baseball had gradually evolved from a gentlemen's club activity, an amateur game played throughout the country in the 1840s and 1850s, into a largely professional sport. Its commercial possibilities, hinted at in the 1860s when crowds showed a willingness to pay to see good players in competition, were furthered by the National Association of Professional Base Ball Players, but the league was torn by problems and it collapsed after the 1875 season. In 1875 one of the league's dominant figures, William Hulbert, decided to take matters into his own hands.

Hulbert, president of the Chicago White Stockings, was a successful wholesale grocer, coal merchant, and a member of the Chicago Board of Trade. He was a forerunner of the "robber barons" of the late nineteenth century's unregulated capitalism. A tough-minded businessman, he was disgusted by the failings of the NAPBBP. After the 1875 season he lured some of the best players away from the Boston team with promises of lucrative contracts. They included Albert Spalding, Boston's best pitcher, Deacon White, a superb third baseman and catcher, and Ross Barnes, a talented shortstop and the best hitter in the league. Hulbert also secured the services of a young future star from Philadelphia, Adrian "Cap" Anson. Anson, at 6 feet, 2 inches and two hundred pounds, was a giant for his time. He would achieve baseball immortality by hitting over .300 in nineteen of his twenty-two years in the majors as well as becoming the first player to achieve three thousand hits. Not all his claims on baseball are positive: he was also partially responsible for the ban against blacks in professional baseball.

Hulbert's motivation was complex. He wanted baseball to be a better-managed sport, he wanted to make money, and he was angry with the game's domination by Eastern teams and owners. A fanatic Chicago booster, he once remarked, "I would rather be a lamppost in Chicago than a millionaire in any other city."

When sportswriters got wind of Hulbert's scheme, there was outrage in the NAPBBP. But Hulbert's plans were well laid. With the aid of Spalding, who was interested in exchanging his player's role for the business side of baseball, and an influential sportswriter for the *Chicago Tribune*, Lewis Meacham, Hulbert enlisted four Midwestern clubs, Chicago, St. Louis, Louisville, and Cincinnati, for his new league. He invited four teams from the East, Philadelphia, Boston, New York, and Hartford, to join his new organization. In February 1876, at a meeting in New York City, the National League of Professional Baseball Clubs, known as the National League for short, was organized. To show his magnanimity, Hulbert stepped aside so that Morgan Bulkeley of the Hartford club could serve as first president of the new league. Bulkeley, whose real interest was a political career, served for one season and then returned to Republican politics in Connecticut. Hulbert took over in 1877 and ran the National League as a benevolent dictator until his death in 1882. Bulkeley is enshrined in the Hall of Fame though he had next to nothing to do with baseball; Hulbert was finally voted in in 1995.

Hulbert, Meacham, and Spalding were ready with new rules based on the experience of past league failures. The membership fee was raised to $100; each team was guaranteed territorial rights for a radius of five miles from its city; new members could be vetoed by two negative votes; and every team would respect other teams' contracts. Only cities with a population of at least 75,000 might be represented. A uniform schedule was drawn up, with each team playing the others ten times. Ticket prices were set at 50 cents, with the visiting team receiving 30 percent of the gate receipts. Hulbert banned Sunday baseball and was adamantly opposed to the sale of beer at games. The new league vowed to police its games to reduce rowdy fan behavior. A league championship would be awarded to the team with the best overall record.

Hulbert wanted to improve the image of baseball among the respectable classes. By the 1870s the game's roughneck reputation was well established. The amateur gentleman's game of the recent past was all but forgotten, though Henry Chadwick tirelessly promoted the older approach to the game in his various sports publications and newspaper articles. By setting a half-dollar minimum price for those exposed to the sun on the bleaching boards (thus the origin of the "bleachers"), Hulbert effectively limited the number of workingmen who could attend games. Since the average wage in the 1880s was about $1 to $3 per day for a blue-collar worker, a fifty-cent charge virtually eliminated them from games. And because games were scheduled for 3:30 on weekday afternoons, few members of the working class could attend.

Hulbert's actions are an almost perfect reflection of the rationalizing changes occurring in American business at the time. Ruthless competition and underhanded business methods were features of the "root hog or die" era of American society. Hulbert was simply applying to baseball the Social Darwinist principles that a Rockefeller, Carnegie, or Morgan would use to consolidate his business and destroy his competition.

The new National League got off to a shaky start as teams dropped out for a variety of reasons, mostly economic.

In the first season alone the Philadelphia and New York teams were expelled for failing to complete their schedules. This robbed the league of its Eastern anchors, but Hulbert didn't care as he wanted to see the Midwest dominate play. This made no economic or geographic sense. The 1877 season included only six teams in the National League, with just two—Hartford and Boston—representing the populous East. At the start of the 1878 season only three of the original teams that launched the new league remained. But that season every one of the six teams played out its schedule for the first time in organized baseball. The instability that had plagued the old National Association continued through the early 1880s, with franchises located in marginal cities such as Providence, Worcester (Massachusetts), Troy (New York), Indianapolis, and Buffalo. This instability partly resulted from difficult economic conditions in the United States in the late 1870s, as the country struggled to recover from the depression of 1873. Few teams showed a profit. The successful Boston club lost money every season from 1876 through 1880.

In 1883 Philadelphia and New York returned to the National League, providing a semblance of geographical balance. The move was in response to the National League's new rival, the American Association. The nucleus of the new league consisted of two clubs expelled from the National League for serious infractions—Cincinnati for allowing the sale of beer, Louisville after losing four players accused of taking bribes—plus the St. Louis club. These three cities joined teams in Philadelphia, Baltimore, and Pittsburgh. The new league was unbalanced, with four of its six founding teams located in the Midwest, but it could boast a franchise in Philadelphia, the second-largest city in America, and that posed a serious challenge to the National League. The spokesman for the American Association, Denny McKnight, a successful Pittsburgh

businessman and baseball enthusiast, pointed out to National
League owners that the American Association represented
cities with a population almost double that of those in the senior league. Four of the six clubs in the American Association
were owned by brewers, which led the league being nicknamed
the Beer Ball League and the Whiskey League. When the National League moved to grant franchises to Philadelphia and
New York, it demonstrated to the American Association that
it was not about to concede the Eastern market. Hulbert's
antipathy toward Eastern clubs had kept the National
League out of the two biggest cities in the nation. His death in
1882 cleared the way for the National League to return to the
East.

## The Reserve Clause

THE AMERICAN ASSOCIATION opened for business in 1882
and was immediately challenged by yet another league, the
Union League, which lasted only a single season, 1884. The
Union League failed because it was poorly financed and because its franchises competed in cities where both the National League and the American Association were already
strong: Boston, Philadelphia, Chicago, and Cincinnati. In desperation the Union League established franchises in cities
such as Altoona (Pennsylvania), which had a small population
base, and Washington, which had yet to prove it could sustain
a professional baseball team. The two established leagues
blacklisted players who jumped to the Union League and refused to recognize the contracts of Union players. The Union
League soon collapsed because it was so poorly organized.

The proliferation of new leagues was a sign of the growing
prosperity of baseball, a prosperity that offset the losses that

most National League teams absorbed during the hard times of the 1870s depression. In the early 1880s baseball owners looked to exploit the nation's newfound love affair with the game. It was big business with the promise of equally big profits. For the players, the three leagues were a godsend, competing for their talents and driving up their salaries. "Revolving," which the National League had tried to eliminate, was still strong, and the lure of new teams tempted players to move around for promises of big paydays. More than thirty players, including such National League stars as Jack Glassop, Charles Sweeney, Tommy Bond, and "Handsome" Tony Mullane, jumped to the newly formed American Association. The threat of instability that had been the bane of baseball still hovered over the sport.

Professional baseball avoided bloody economic warfare by two means. First, the presidents of the National League, A. G. Mills, and Denny McKnight of the American Association, hammered out a peace treaty known as the National Agreement, whereby the two leagues agreed to respect each other's rules and procedures. The leadership in these negotiations was taken by Mills, who in 1882 had succeeded the combative Hulbert. Mills used quiet diplomacy as well as timely reminders of the problems that had destroyed the old league in order to bring together the often unruly businessmen who ran baseball. Harold Seymour argues that the creation of the National Agreement marked the beginning of organized baseball because it was the first workable formula for regulating competition among players and leagues that stood the test of time.

Second, and equally important, was the adoption of the reserve clause by professional baseball. The idea of permanently "reserving" players to one team developed in the mid-1870s to combat "revolving," especially players jumping from one team to another during the season. Clearly this practice was driving up players' salaries; a way had to be found to control costs. Given the sanctity of the idea of contract in nineteenth-century law, an arrangement whereby a player was bound to his club for the duration of his career seemed both possible and legal.

The reserve clause was first adopted by the National League in 1879 at the instigation of Arthur Soden, president of the Boston Red Stockings. Each club was allowed to designate five players who were so important to them that their services would be held by the team until the player was sold, traded, or released. All other clubs bound themselves to respect the contracts of these players. The number of players "reserved" was gradually extended over the years to eleven in 1883, twelve in 1886, and finally the entire team in 1889. A player jumping his contract now found that he was unemployable. Many players tested the new principle over the next few years, only to discover that they were effectively blacklisted and that baseball management had finally stumbled on a way to regulate salary costs. The National Agreement and the reserve clause saved baseball in the 1880s but at a price: the game became a monopoly which reduced its workers to a state of high-salaried peonage.

Baseball wages rose slowly in the prosperous 1880s until the average player's salary reached $1,600 per year, with the stars such as Cap Anson making $2,500 and Mike "King" Kelly even earning $5,000 when his endorsements were added. Of course, many players worked in the off-season, a phenomenon that persisted in baseball until the big contracts of the 1970s transformed the salary structure of the sport. Players drifted to largely unskilled jobs as bartenders, pool hall attendants, carpenters, and teamsters. Still, baseball salaries were vastly better than those of laborers in the country. In the

1880s an industrial worker's average annual income was approximately $650, and unemployment ran about 10 percent. With players able to make almost three times that income, even though the average career rarely exceeded six years, no wonder that for many young men baseball seemed like a golden opportunity.

### *Baseball's First Heroes*

THE 1880S saw baseball mature both as a sport and as a business. The refinement of play rapidly exceeded what had been achieved a decade earlier. In 1881 the pitching distance was increased from forty-five to fifty feet. After various experiments, including a nine-ball walk, it was decided that four balls would constitute a free pass to first base, and that the pitcher would now throw overhand (1884). While most pitchers still relied on speed, the change of pace and the curve—easier to throw overhand—became commonplace. In 1887 the strike zone was defined as between the shoulders and the knees. The search for balance between offense and defense continued while almost all players adopted gloves by the end of the decade. Errors declined as a result. In 1889 the National League hit .264 while the league earned run average (ERA) was 4.02. For the American Association the comparable figures were .262 and 3.84. Almost a century later, in 1987, the figures for the National League were .261 and 4.08, a remarkable measure of continuity unmatched in any other sport. The game of baseball in the 1880s would be instantly recognizable to any fan today.

Baseball may have been the national pastime since the 1860s, but it produced its first great stars only in the 1880s. Other than politicians and entertainers, the greatest players of that era were among the first real celebrities in American history. While John L. Sullivan, the heavyweight champion, may have been the best-known athlete in America at the time, some baseball players were not far behind. If little boys and young men had idols in the 1880s, they were likely to be baseball players. A poster advertising the Allen and Ginter Tobacco Company in 1887 announced that fifty "World Champion" cards could be found in each pack of its cigarettes. Ten of the fifty were baseball players, including Cap Anson, Tim Keefe, King Kelly, and John Montgomery Ward, a testament to the game's hold on the male imagination.

The most admired baseball player was probably Anson, though the public was unaware of his darker side, especially his racism. Anson was a great player and manager, if not a particularly lovable personality. He had a huge following in Chicago and deserved his fame as one of baseball's first heroes. The first player to reach three thousand hits for his career, he finished with a lifetime batting average of .334, a figure which ranks twentieth in the history of baseball.

Anson's role in establishing baseball's color barrier is controversial. Blacks played professional baseball at all levels in the 1870s and 1880s, with a handful, such as pitcher George Stovey and infielder Frank Grant, achieving star status. Stovey was one of the hardest-throwing lefthanders in the International League while Grant led the same league in batting in 1887 with a .366 average. But by the mid-1880s baseball was beginning to be influenced by the racial segregation that was spreading out of the South into all parts of the nation. Sol White, the first black baseball writer of any consequence, identified 1887 as the year when baseball joined the nation in segregating the races on the ball field. That year Anson refused to take his White Stockings team on the field in an exhibition game against Newark of the International League with its black battery of Stovey and Moses Fleetwood Walker.

That same year a League of Colored Base Ball Clubs opened in six cities, including Pittsburgh, Philadelphia, Louisville, New York, Baltimore, and Boston. The existing major leagues recognized the Colored League, as it was called, by admitting them to the National Agreement. Unfortunately the new league collapsed in mid-season, a fate that had beset the major leagues in the recent past. It would take another thirty years before a new effort would be made to create a separate league for blacks—Rube Foster's Negro National League that began in the 1920s.

The first player to approach mythic or superstar status was Mike "King" Kelly, who played for Anson in Chicago and was later traded to Boston where he was an even bigger hero to the large Irish community. Kelly was among the first of the great Irish American ballplayers who would dominate the sport in the next two decades. It is interesting to note that the first two sports heroes in America in the 1880s, Sullivan and Kelly, were Irish Catholics at a time when anti-Catholicism was a powerful force, especially in the Midwest. The popularity of the American Protective Society, with its message of hatred for Catholics and immigrants, peaked in the late 1880s and early 1890s, just as Irish Americans came to the fore in baseball. For the first but not the last time, sport served to ease the path to acceptance of an outside group by the larger society.

Kelly possessed a special charisma about the way he played the game—recklessly but with flair and a sense of fun that brought fans into the park. Essentially an outfielder and catcher, the rawboned 5-foot, 10-inch 170-pounder could not match Anson's hitting credentials, though Kelly won two batting titles, once hitting an astounding .388. What set him apart was his uproarious approach to the game. He was extremely fast and, according to most reports, one of the first base runners to develop the hook slide as a way of avoiding the fielder's tag. When he reached base the fans would cheer, "Slide, Kelly, slide," and he would do so with a flourish. As a catcher, he would drop his mask in front of home plate on a close play to deflect the incoming runner's slide. Kelly also was one of the first athletes to capitalize on his fame through advertising endorsements and by appearing on the stage. Unfortunately he shared another quality typical of many players of his time: alcoholism.

In the 1880s alcohol was baseball's drug of choice. The American Association in particular had a reputation for drunken fans, not surprising given the role that brewers played in the league. Perhaps the twenty-five-cent admission plus Sunday baseball attracted a lower class of fan to the American Association than the National League, which featured neither of these allures. The St. Louis Browns of the American Association, owned by the eccentric brewer Chris Von der Ahe, provided a beer garden in the ballpark to satisfy the thirsty fan. Since many players came from Irish and German working-class backgrounds, they tended to drink. The number of functioning alcoholics in baseball was in fact surprising. In his *Historical Abstract of Baseball,* the baseball guru Bill James has a section for each decade labeled "Drinking Men." In the 1880s that section includes not only Kelly but also such stars as Charlie Sweeney, pitcher Mickey Welch, and slugging outfielder Pete Browning.

Kelly's benders were legendary. When asked if he drank during a game, he replied, "It depends on the length of the game." His career ended in the early 1890s, and he died of chronic alcoholism while not yet thirty-seven years old.

An evocative story is told of his last illness, pneumonia complicated by his drinking. As he was being carried on a stretcher to the hospital, attendants carelessly dropped him to the floor. Kelly is supposed to have remarked, "This is my last slide."

An all-star team for the 1880s would contain players who could compare to the best players in any decade in baseball history. Dan Brouthers and Roger Connor, who played largely in the National League, were among baseball's first great sluggers. Both men were big for their time, with Connor at 6 feet, 3 inches and 220 pounds qualifying as a giant. Essentially first basemen, both men established that position as one for power hitters. Brouthers finished with a lifetime batting average of .343, which ranks him ninth overall, while Connor drove in more than a thousand runs and finished his career with a batting average of .318 and 2,480 hits.

Sam Thompson, who played with Detroit and Philadelphia in the National League between 1880 and 1898, was another big man—6 feet, 2 inches and 207 pounds. He was probably the greatest outfielder of his time. In an era when home runs were rare, he hit 128 in his career including 20 in one season. He drove in 1,299 runs in his career.

Buck Ewing, a catcher, established this position as crucial to the success of any team. While he did not reach the statistical levels of Connor, Brouthers, or Thompson, Ewing was one of the most admired players of his era. He had a strong throwing arm and handled pitchers effortlessly. He was baseball's first great backstop, defining catching play for decades.

On the mound the greatest pitchers of the day were Tim Keefe, John Clarkson, and Charles Radbourn. In a twelve-year career, Clarkson won 326 games while losing just 177. His career ERA was 2.81. Keefe, like Clarkson, was a righthander and one of the game's first great fastball pitchers. He struck out 2,500 batters in his career, including 300 in a season three times. His 344 victories rank him eighth overall in baseball history.

Radbourn's statistics are not as impressive as Clarkson's or Keefe's, but he was regarded as the hardest thrower of his time. A little righthander with the delightful nickname "Old Hoss," he was just 5 feet, 9 inches and 168 pounds. Radbourn threw powerfully, with a kind of last-second leap toward the batter. In 1884 he struck out 441 batters for Providence in the National League. He also won 60 games against only 12 losses that season, starting and completing 73 games—figures not likely ever to be matched. He died at age 42 of the last stages of syphilis, paresis of the brain.

These players were hero-worshipped by fans all over the country, especially by young boys who tried to copy their stances or style of play. Baseball in the 1880s indelibly impressed itself into the nation's imagination.

Another sign of baseball's growing popularity was the astounding success of a piece of verse about the travails of a great hitter, "Casey at the Bat." In June 1888 the poem appeared in William Randolph Hearst's *San Francisco Examiner.* It drew little attention until it was incorporated into the act of a music-hall monologist named De Wolf Hopper. In August 1888 Hopper recited "Casey" in New York before an audience that included ballplayers from the Chicago White Stockings and New York Giants. They raved about the poem, which Hopper wisely made a standard part of his act. He later estimated that had he recited the poem more than ten thousand times over the course of his career. It became one of the defining pieces of American popular culture. Casey joined "John Henry," "Johnny Appleseed," and "Paul Bunyan" as icons of American folk culture. The poem with its pathos, sentimentalism, and trick ending—almost perfectly mirrors the

hold that baseball had on the nation's imagination at the end
of the nineteenth century. The reader or listener is led to expect Casey to hit a home run. Instead the mighty Casey
strikes out, and there is no joy in Mudville. Every baseball
"fan"—the word came into popular use in the 1880s, most
likely coined by the manager and scout T. P. Sullivan, and
short for "fanatic"—knew the agony of seeing his hero fail in
the clutch. This situation perfectly captures the innocence
and naiveté of America at the time. The fame of "Casey at the
Bat" was also linked to the ease of reciting it at a time when
dramatic readings were enormously popular.

"Casey at the Bat" was filmed by Thomas Edison in 1898
and in 1927 was made into a feature-length silent film by
Paramount Pictures, starring Wallace Beery. Walt Disney did
a cartoon version of Casey in 1946 in "Make Mine Music." The
poem has never been out of print. Interestingly, the author, a
Massachusetts newspaperman and textile-mill owner, with a
proper Yankee name, Ernest Lawrence Thayer, first published
the poem anonymously. He came to detest it and the fame it
brought him. "All I ask," he once said, "is never to be re-
minded of it again."

Thayer was asked who was his model for Casey. He never
provided a name, and many players came forward over the
years to claim they were the inspiration for Casey. Dan Casey,
a pitcher in the major leagues from 1884 to 1890, argued for
years that Thayer used him as a model. It doesn't seem likely,
given the fact that Dan Casey was primarily a pitcher with a
lifetime batting average of .162 and one home run. A better
possibility would be King Kelly. Kelly shared many of Casey's
attributes—boastful, proud, and a great hitter. Kelly played
for Boston after 1887, thus Thayer might have seen his exploits.

If "Casey at the Bat" was the most famous piece of popular baseball literature, it wasn't the first. Throughout the 1880s books about baseball, mostly aimed at the young, appeared regularly. Mike Kelly's *"Play Ball"; Stories of the Diamond Field* and John Montgomery Ward's *Base-ball. How to Become a Player* were successes and the beginnings of a trend in baseball literature that would continue for the rest of the sport's history.

Another sign of the game's popularity was the proliferation of baseball-oriented periodicals. The *New York Clipper* and *Sporting Life* had been around for years, devoting considerable space to baseball. The Spink brothers, Charles and Alfred, founded the *Sporting News* in St. Louis in 1886 with a special dedication to baseball and a strong Midwestern orientation. With its emphasis on statistics and its deadly earnest coverage of baseball, the *Sporting News* soon outpaced its rivals and became known, somewhat egotistically, as the "Bible of Baseball." It held the field as the leading baseball weekly until the demand for more diversified and stimulating sports coverage led to the founding of *Sports Illustrated* in 1954 by Time Inc.

Along with the weekly sports papers, baseball also spawned another type of publication—the yearly almanac or guide. First in the field was *Spalding's Official Base Ball Guide,* which began publication in 1877 and was edited by Henry Chadwick until his death in 1908. Spalding cleverly used his popular guide to advertise and market his sporting goods. His rival, A. J. Reach, joined the competition in 1883 with his *Official Base Ball Guide.*

Reach's sporting goods company was also Spalding's greatest competition in the sale of related sports products. Reach claimed to have invented a machine that produced high-quality tightly bound baseballs which were superior to any others. Taking a page from the success of A. Montgomery

Ward, whose company launched catalog sales in Chicago in 1872, Reach was the industry leader in direct-mail sales. In 1889 he sold his interests in his company to Spalding and took an executive position with his former competitor. Reach's products, including his baseball, continued to be marketed by Spalding under his name and in 1902 his ball was adopted as the official baseball of the newly formed American League.

### The Players' "Strike"

THE 1880S proved to be baseball's first golden age. The National Agreement had brought a tenuous peace between the National League and the American Association, enabling them easily to turn back the challenge of the Union League. Baseball thrived in the prosperous decade, with such teams as Chicago, New York, and Boston turning profits of $100,000 per season, a phenomenal sum in those days. One sign of baseball's prosperity was the construction of better baseball parks. Jerry-built wooden parks began to give way to more solid arenas. The Polo Grounds of the mid-1880s resembles a small city park. It easily held crowds of 20,000 or more, and people could park their carriages beyond the outfield fences and watch the games. Chicago's Lakefront Stadium, built in 1877 after the Great Fire, by 1883 seated 10,000. It included 18 private boxes. The most impressive of the new parks was to be found in Philadelphia, where A. J. Reach, owner of the Phillies, in 1887 built the first steel-and-brick ballpark, Baker Bowl. Constructed at the then enormous sum of $101,000, Baker Bowl could seat 12,500. Ballparks could still be thrown together in a matter of days or weeks for sums under $10,000. Since they were wooden affairs, they burned down with frequency.

Baseball's prosperity was enhanced by informal playoffs called world championships, played between the winners of the National League and the American Association beginning in 1882 and lasting until 1891 when the two leagues renewed warfare. There were no playoffs in 1883 because of league disputes. In 1885 Chris Von der Ahe's St. Louis Browns, champions of the American Association, challenged Cap Anson's White Stockings to a post-season test to see who had the best baseball team. Games were played not just in Chicago and St. Louis but throughout cities in both leagues. The outcome was declared a tie, and the two teams divided the championship purse of $1,000 put up by a journal, the *Mirror of American Sports.*

The next season, when the same two teams won their league titles, another playoff series was arranged, this time on a winner-take-all basis at Anson's insistence. St. Louis won $13,910 when the winning run was scored on a botched pickoff play. Anson was embarrassed and furious, Von der Ahe immensely pleased. He had offered a side bet of $10,000 that Anson rejected. Later it was rumored that the players on both squads had agreed among themselves to divide the proceeds.

The playoffs clearly showed the supremacy of the National League. Its teams won four championships and lost one, with one tie. In 1889 the second game of the series between the Giants and Brooklyn drew 16,200 fans, a huge crowd for those days and a sure sign of baseball's prosperity. The 1887 playoffs between the Detroit Wolverines and the St. Louis Browns attracted 51,500 fans.

Baseball attendance figures are unreliable until the twentieth century, but it appears that the game attracted reasonably good crowds throughout the 1880s. Attendance peaked in 1889 when the two major leagues drew approximately 3 million fans. The National League figure was 1,353,000, with the remainder being drawn by the American Association with its lower ticket prices and Sunday games. The New York Giants led National League attendance with 201,000 fans while the Brooklyn Bridegrooms of the American Association drew 353,000, including the largest crowd in major league history to that date, 20,914. These figures compare favorably with baseball attendance after the formation of the two major leagues early in the twentieth century. For example, in 1902 only one team in the National League, St. Louis, and one in the American League, Philadelphia, outdrew the 1889 Brooklyn Bridegrooms. The Brooklyn club of the National League did not top the Bridegrooms' figure until 1916.

But hanging over this prosperous period for baseball was a shadow. As salaries rose in the 1880s, some owners sought ways to control expenses. The reserve clause had stabilized the game, but costs continued to rise. One idea was to classify all players in categories, each with a salary limit. In 1885 the owners imposed a limit of $2,000 for a star player, but apparently it was largely ignored. Players were doing well and the game was thriving, but many players felt they were not sharing in baseball's financial success. They were especially angry at blacklisting, which not only deprived them of their jobs but also demeaned them. Borrowing a concept from sociology and history, David Voigt argues that baseball players were suffering from "status deprivation."

An interesting theory, but most baseball players didn't fit the mold of upwardly mobile middle classes who saw their position threatened by classes from below. Professional baseball players increasingly were drawn from the ranks of the artisan class; they were the sons of immigrants or were lower-class city boys who had succeeded in an occupation where the em-

phasis was on skill and talent, not background. The new ownership of baseball was more economically aggressive than the
gentleman owners of the past, and this angered players who
were passed around from club to club without any benefit ac-
cruing to them.

In response to this situation, John Montgomery Ward, a
star shortstop for the New York Giants and a practicing
lawyer, began in 1885 to organize a players' union, called the
National Brotherhood of Base Ball. Among the first to join
were fellow Giant stars Roger Connor, Buck Ewing, and
pitcher Tim Keefe. Ward's idea was to be ready for a confrontation with baseball management if salary limits were imposed. By the end of 1887 the Brotherhood had enrolled
approximately 107 members from the National League and 30
from the American Association, enough to demonstrate that
the Brotherhood was real. National League owners, led by
Spalding, at first negotiated with the Brotherhood, but in fact
they were just buying time.

After the 1888 season Spalding organized another tour,
this time to show baseball not just to England but to the
world. Spalding wanted to spread the gospel of Americanism
by introducing baseball around the globe. He also believed
that the tour would make a tidy profit. The tour enlisted players from the two major leagues and effectively forestalled any
confrontation over salaries for the time being.

The tour was a considerable success. It started with a series of games throughout the western United States which
produced sufficient revenue to pay for the trip across the Pa-
cific to Australia and New Zealand. After games in Ceylon,
Egypt, Italy, and France, Spalding's squad played eleven
games in Great Britain. Despite costs of $50,000, the
1888–1889 tour turned a modest profit. Spalding called it "the
greatest event in the modern history of sport."

Ward was part of the tour. When he returned in early 1889 he discovered that the baseball owners, led by John T. Brush of the Indianapolis club of the National League, had imposed the salary scale. All players were classified A through E, with salaries ranging from $2,500 down to $1,500. Ward was furious, and when he demanded talks with ownership he was told there "was nothing to discuss." He counseled the Brotherhood to play out the 1889 season and plan for action the next year.

Ward's group now approached wealthy businessmen with an interest in sport to back a new league for the 1890 season. It wasn't difficult to find investors, for baseball's popularity and financial success attracted men who hoped to make a killing. The costs of starting a new league were low; a ballpark could be thrown up in a matter of weeks or even days, and the Brotherhood had plenty of quality players available. Among the businessmen that Ward approached were Colonel Edwin McAlpin, the New York hotel tycoon, and Al Johnson, a rich traction magnate in Cleveland. Johnson was politically well connected: his brother was the reform mayor of Cleveland, Tom "Golden Rule" Johnson.

Shortly after the 1889 season ended, the new Players League was organized at a meeting in New York City. What made the new league unique was the alliance of owners and players to share power and profits equally. Game receipts would be divided equally with the home team keeping the concessions revenues. To provide stability, all players signed three-year contracts based on their pay for the 1889 season. The reserve clause was abrogated, blacklisting was outlawed, and the players agreed to police themselves on issues of gambling and alcoholism. The new league targeted the National League and tried to keep the American Association neutral, but this strategy eventually failed as teams in the new league began to offer lucrative contracts to American Association players.

It was decided to challenge the National League by putting teams in seven of its cities: New York, Boston, Brooklyn, Philadelphia, Pittsburgh, Cleveland, and Chicago. The eighth franchise was granted to Buffalo. The National League responded by declaring baseball war. Spalding, with John Day of the Giants and John Rogers of Philadelphia, chaired a three-man committee to direct the struggle. Spalding branded the Brotherhood—in words that resonated in those anti-union days—as "an oath bound, secret organization of strikers." This was provocative language, for the United States had just emerged from a period of serious strikes. Twice as many strikes had occurred in 1886 as in any year in the nation's history. The worst of them took place in Chicago, where a massive protest by more than eighty thousand workers clamoring for the eight-hour day culminated in the Haymarket Affair, in which seven policemen were killed and more than sixty people injured when a bomb was thrown. Labor militancy grew through the late 1880s, and it was easy to brand unions as hotbeds of anarchism when workers tried to share in the nation's prosperity.

Baseball's largely middle-class audience was unsympathetic to strikes or unionism. But both of the leading baseball weeklies, the *Sporting News* and *Sporting Life of New York*, supported the players. The *Sporting News* even looked forward to the battle for supremacy between the two new leagues on good Social Darwinist grounds: the war would purge baseball of its weaker elements.

Spalding shrewdly avoided attacking the players, whom he knew baseball would need whenever what he regarded as the "strike" ended. Instead he and his allies tried to divide the players from the businessmen who backed the new league.

Branding the backers as pirates who didn't have the interest of baseball at heart, the National League gradually drove a wedge between them and the players.

The 1890 season was a disaster for baseball. Three major leagues and twenty-four teams were too many. The public was disgusted by the squabbling, and fans stayed away from games. Although all the leagues claimed inflated attendance figures, the reality was grim. *Reach's Guide* for 1890 listed the National League as drawing 814,000 fans, the new Players League 981,000. But the real figures were shocking. In the Players League, Cleveland averaged 927 and Buffalo 942 fans per game, in the National League, New York drew 919 and Pittsburgh 414 per game. Everyone lost money, though accurate figures are difficult to come by. National League losses were estimated at more than $300,000, a truly staggering sum in those days.

The National League finally prevailed in this struggle, dragging along a seriously weakened American Association. The senior circuit was better financed, had superior executive leadership, and had established itself in the public mind as baseball's premier league. Before the 1890 season ended, some of the businessmen who ran the Players League, supposedly with the cooperation of the players themselves, were looking for a way out. The approach they took was to try to gain admission to the National League, even if the price was selling out the new league.

Talks held after the 1890 season led to the collapse of the Players League. In November 1890 it dissolved in a sea of debts and recriminations among owners and players. Spalding and other National League owners were magnanimous and promised there would be no recriminations against the players. The reserve clause was retained, and limitations on player's salaries continued. Even John Montgomery Ward, the

Brotherhood leader, was welcomed back. The owners realized that they needed the players to regain the confidence of baseball's fans.

Professional baseball had survived its first real crisis with the sport intact. Management had shown that they, not the players, ran the game and the business of baseball. Their triumph would prove to be short-lived.

*From left, Christy Mathewson, John McGraw, and "Iron Man" Joe McGinnity of the New York Giants.*

# Chapter 3

# COMING OF AGE, 1891–1908

THE PLAYERS LEAGUE DEFEAT was engineered by the owners of the National League with the American Association standing by. Within a year the American Association would be a memory. The sorting out of returning players left the National League with all the best talent. A failure to include talented players such as Louis Bierbauer and Harry Stovey on the American Association's list of reserved players led them to jump to National League teams. For taking Bierbauer and Stovey, Pittsburgh was accused of acting like pirates, a name that stuck to the team. American Association protests were rejected with contempt by National League officials who now believed the rival league was doomed.

The American Association reacted by rejecting the National Agreement and trying to raid National League rosters, but without much success. Players were wary of another Players League fiasco. They were happy to be playing baseball and not being blacklisted.

War between the two leagues was scarcely an even contest. The National League had teams in the best cities while the American Association struggled in places such as Milwau-

kee and Columbus. Attendance sagged for both leagues after
the Players League folded, but the Association, with its
twenty-five-cent seats, was less able to stand the competition.

After the 1891 season the American Association owners
sued for peace and agreed to break up their league. Four of
their most successful teams joined the National League:
Washington, Baltimore, Louisville, and St. Louis. Chris Von
der Ahe played a key role in brokering the negotiations. In return for being allowed to establish a franchise in St. Louis,
where he had had great success in the 1880s, he helped convince his fellow Association owners to disband.

The collapse of the American Association distorted the
judgment of National League owners. They became arrogant
and complacent after their successes in the baseball wars.
But their arrogance would soon turn to bewilderment as the
nation drifted into the worst depression in its history.

The depression of the 1890s had its roots in an agricul-
tural crisis that began in 1887 as farm prices collapsed
throughout the Midwest and South. Soon a new political
movement called populism emerged to lead the farming
classes in revolt against their perceived oppressors: the big
cities of the East, Wall Street bankers, and new immigrants
who were accused of taking American jobs. In 1893 the precipitous decline in farm prices caught up to the rest of the nation. Banks collapsed; businesses cut production and laid off
workers. In 1894 the unemployment rate soared to 18.4 percent, the highest in American history until the Great Depression of the 1930s, and it remained above 10 percent until 1898.

After two terrible internal wars, baseball was unable to
avoid the consequences of the nation's economic collapse. The
depression plunged professional baseball into a crisis in some
ways worse than the league wars.

Attendance plummeted throughout the decade, partly

spawned by disgust with baseball's squabbles, partly related to economic problems, and after 1893 connected to the inanity of a twelve-team league. The two major leagues had drawn 3 million fans in 1889, baseball's best year. Five years later the figure was 1,850,000, a decline of 38 percent. As late as 1897, as the depression began to fade, National League attendance was 2,883,000, still 117,000 short of its record year.

The twelve-team league set up in 1892 presented serious problems that baseball had not foreseen, particularly the lack of meaningful competition. A twelve-team league meant that the gap between the first- and last-place teams might be so enormous that many fans would lose interest. In the first year of the new league, the champion Boston Beaneaters' lead over the last three teams in the division was 45½, 46, and 54 games. In 1898 the gap between the top and bottom teams was 63½ games; the next year Brooklyn's lead over the last-place Cleveland Spiders was an incredible 84 games. That year Cleveland won just 20 games against 132 losses, a .129 record and the worst team average in baseball history. As a result of all these factors, during the 1890s some teams averaged just 2,000 to 3,000 fans per game.

Even to obtuse management, this situation couldn't continue. The National League tried various expedients throughout the decade to generate interest in baseball. In 1892 it used a split-season format; but the league drew 300,000 fewer fans in the second half than the first. (Baseball would flirt with this idea almost 90 years later, after the players strike of 1981, with equally disastrous results.)

In 1893 the owners decided to increase the role of offense in hopes of luring fans back to the game, a method that would be used in the future with some success. Pitching had dominated baseball, even after the pitching distance had been increased to 50 feet. In 1892 the batting champion hit .335, the top slugging percentage was .495, and the home run leader hit 13. That season there were six 30-game winners and eleven 20-game winners.

In 1893 the pitching distance was increased by another 10½ feet to the present 60 feet, 6 inches. Baseball offense now increased dramatically. The top batting average rose to .380 and the slugging percentage to .583, while the home run leader hit 19. The number of 30-game winners dropped to four; 20-game winners declined to six. The league batting average rose from .245 to .280, and there were twenty-eight .300 hitters versus nine the year before. The league ERA rose from 3.28 to 4.60, the greatest increase in baseball history. Yet all this offense failed to turn out the fans. Baseball remained in the doldrums.

In an effort to drum up interest, National League owners decided to revive the playoff idea used with success in the 1880s. Since there was only one league now, this meant some form of interleague championship. In the 1892 split season, the winner of the first half, Cleveland, played the second-half champion, Boston. The first game ended in a tie, then Boston swept the next five. The split-season format was dropped the next season.

In 1893 there was no playoff. After the 1893 season a Pittsburgh businessman named William Temple offered the National League a deal. He would donate a beautiful silver trophy, thirty inches high with a pitcher throwing a ball etched in relief, worth $800 and made by the celebrated New York jeweler A. E. Thrall, if baseball would establish a genuine playoff. The first team to win three series would get to keep the trophy permanently. National League owners liked the plan, as did the players for whom it would mean extra money. The winning team would take 65 percent of the gate receipts, the loser 35 percent, so there would be a reason for

the players to try to win. (In fact players on both teams con-
spired to divide the gate receipts equally.) It was decided that
the first-place team would play the second-place finisher in a
best-of-seven series.

The Temple Cup series was played for four years beginning in 1894 but with only limited success. In three of these
years the second-place team won the series. None of the playoffs was competitive or very exciting; two ended in five games
while the other two were four-game sweeps. While it is difficult to obtain accurate attendance figures, it appears that
only the 1894 series, won by the second-place New York Giants over the champion Baltimore Orioles, attracted a significant number of fans—55,000. Later playoff games were often
sparsely attended. Game four of the 1896 sweep of Baltimore
over the second-place Cleveland Spiders attracted only 1,200
fans. Temple withdrew his offer after the 1897 season, to the
relief of baseball owners who saw no profit in playoffs. For the
next six years baseball lacked a playoff format.

The National League also suffered in the 1890s from the
fact that two teams, the Baltimore Orioles and Boston
Beaneaters, easily dominated the competition. These two
teams won pennants every year after the collapse of the American Association until 1899 when Brooklyn broke their string.
Both the Orioles and the Beaneaters were superb teams which
combined great pitching, solid hitting, and sturdy defense.
They specialized in the kind of "inside" baseball—hitting and
running, stealing bases, tight defense, and strong pitching—
that dominated the game until the long-ball era arrived in the
1920s. Led by stars such as John McGraw, Willie Keeler, and
Hughie Jennings, the Orioles played some of the most aggressive baseball of the era. In fact, some observers thought the
Orioles' brand of reckless, roughhouse baseball helped drive
fans away from the game. They cheated and bent the rules by

such ploys as substituting soft used balls when the opposition
came to bat.

The umpire was a special target of the Orioles' abuse.
John Heydler, an umpire in the 1890s and later president of
the National League, blamed the Orioles for polluting baseball with their brand of play. "They were mean, vicious, ready
at any time to maim a rival player or an umpire," he wrote.
"The worst of it was they got by with much of brow beating
and hooliganism. Other clubs patterned after them and I feel
the lot of the umpire never was worse than in the years when
the Orioles were flying high."

Connie Mack, the Philadelphia baseball great who played
and managed against the Orioles, said there were "no gentlemen" on the team. Still, five of these Orioles were eventually
elected to the Hall of Fame. Two, McGraw and Hughie Jennings, became among the best, most imaginative managers in
the first decades of baseball in the modern era—McGraw for
thirty years for the New York Giants, Jennings for fourteen
years for the Detroit Tigers. It was Jennings who found a way
to harness the talent of a driven Georgian named Ty Cobb.

The Boston Beaneaters were a tough crew too, but they
also boasted some of the great hitters of the decade. They included Bobby Lowe, the first player to hit four homers in a
game; Jimmy Collins, the greatest third baseman of his era;
Hugh Duffy, a fine outfielder who hit .438 in 1894; and "Sliding Billy" Hamilton, the greatest base-stealer in an age of
great base runners. But Boston also had some of the greatest
pitchers of the decade in Charles "Kid" Nichols and Vic Willis.
Possessed of a rubber arm and a blazing fastball, Nichols went
on to win 360 games, including an incredible seven consecutive 30-win seasons. When people think of 1890s baseball the
Orioles get most of the attention, but Boston was the better
team.

Many baseball writers blamed baseball's problems in the 1890s on the influence of Irish American players. They were said to have corrupted the gentleman's game. Certainly Irish players such as McGraw contributed to the bad image of baseball in the decade, but one of the worst practitioners, the hard-drinking, brawling Patsy Tebeau of Cleveland wasn't Irish.

In the midst of the 1890s depression, and once they were sure they had beaten back all rival leagues, National League owners ruthlessly cut their payrolls by 30 to 40 percent. A "gentleman's agreement" placed limits of $2,400 on players' salaries and $30,000 on team payrolls. The owners were desperate for profits. While these limits were not always adhered to, they had the effect of lowering salaries across the board. Lists of salaries for Phillies players show that the highest-paid players in 1892 received $3,400 to $3,500. For the 1893 season everyone on the team was cut to $1,800. These reductions angered the players who between 1889 and 1892 had made good money. The next time the National League was challenged by an upstart league, the players remembered the cuts.

Baseball's problems were also complicated in the 1890s by the first serious challenge to the sport's domination in America. Competition for leisure time and dollars now appeared in the form of bicycling, the popular rage of the decade, and in the emergence of such new sports as basketball, volleyball, and college football. Both basketball and volleyball caught on quickly and were played with enormous enthusiasm in gymnasiums and the newly organized YMCAs throughout the country.

Basketball, not long after its invention in 1891 by James Naismith, gained a large following. In 1895 Luther Gulick, one of the key figures in the YMCA movement, remarked on the fanaticism of basketball fans. "In several places," he wrote, "the game was played with such fierceness . . . the crowds who looked on so boisterous and rowdyish, and the bad feeling developed between teams so extreme that the game has been abolished in toto."

In the 1890s college football, which had been around since the 1870s, began to catch the imagination of the better-educated sports fan. A Princeton-Yale game in the depression year of 1893 attracted fifty thousand fans, some of whom paid five dollars a ticket, an astronomical sum in those days. Football had to overcome a reputation for sheer brutality, including numerous deaths from on-field play such as gang tackling and piling on. Despite its roughness, football had to wait another generation until the blue-collar fan was attracted to the sport. In 1888 a sign of football's growing popularity was the player and coach Walter Camp's selection of his first All-American football team. This became a yearly ritual that attracted interest to the sport. Baseball did not duplicate this public relations ploy for years, a sign of a loss of imagination in a game that had dominated the sports scene.

## Byron "Ban" Johnson and the American League

BASEBALL DIFFICULTIES in the 1890s were not all self-inflicted, but internal squabbles cast a pall over the sport's future. It was clear by the end of the decade that twelve teams were too many for one league, yet the more sensible concept of dividing the league into two divisions failed to be adopted for lack of leadership. It also hurt the league that some owners bought into more than one franchise. A. G. Spalding ran the White Sox but also owned a part-interest in the New York Giants. The Brooklyn Superbas, champs of the 1899 season, were partly owned by Ned Hanlon of the Baltimore Orioles.

John Brush, owner of Cincinnati, also held stock in the New York Giants.

Nick Young, baseball's kindly "Uncle Nick," the titular president of the National League, wasn't the man to force twelve willful owners to act as a unit. An amiable figurehead, Young was dominated by powerful club owners such as Spalding, Brush, and especially Andrew Freeman of the New York Giants. Freeman's behavior was symptomatic of the problems of ownership at this time. A wealthy real estate tycoon and traction magnate with political connections in New York City, he had purchased the Giants in 1895 for $50,000. Almost immediately he was at loggerheads with his own players while even his fellow owners came to dislike him. He drove his best pitcher, twenty-three-game winner Amos Rusie, out of baseball in 1896 by cutting his salary two hundred dollars over petty issues. His players hated him and referred to baseball's first Jewish owner as a "sheeny." An aggressively litigious man, Freeman at one time had twenty-two libel suits pending against the *New York Sun*.

By 1899 National League owners recognized that major renovations were necessary if baseball were to survive. Some teams such as Louisville were in desperate financial straits; others such as Cleveland were struggling at the gate and on the field. Owners considered reviving the old American Association in order to create the natural rivalry that in the 1880s had led to profits. But it made little sense to establish a new league when the existing twelve-team league wasn't making money. More and more the idea of returning to the older eight-team arrangement made sense. But while National League owners squabbled among themselves over what to do, initiative passed out of their hands to a dangerous rival.

In November 1893 the thirty-year-old sports editor of the *Cincinnati Commercial Gazette*, Byron Bancroft "Ban"

Johnson, was asked by the owners of the Western League to take over that troubled organization. The league had teams scattered throughout the Midwest in Kansas City, Milwaukee, Minneapolis, Toledo, Grand Rapids, Detroit, and Sioux City. It played a good brand of baseball, though it was clearly a cut below major-league status.

The son of a college teacher, Johnson was a typical product of late-nineteenth-century America. Motivated by Horatio Alger ideas of success, he believed hard work could overcome all obstacles and lead to fame and riches. He was a huge fellow, a three-hundred-pound smoking, hard-drinking, humorless man with slicked hair parted in the middle and a pince-nez perched on his nose. Johnson knew what baseball needed. Good-quality play on the field, fair umpiring, an end to rowdy behavior, and no gambling would ensure the future of the game while also guaranteeing profits. He quickly turned the Western League around, earning it the reputation of being the best-run minor league in baseball.

But Johnson had bigger ideas: he wanted to challenge the monopoly of the National League. In 1899, when National League owners approached him about reviving the American Association, Johnson turned them down. In October that year he changed the name of the Western League to the American League, reflecting the surging nationalism of a people who had just fought and won "a splendid little war" against Spain. The United States was in a patriotic mood at the turn of the century, a mood that would soon be personified by a new president, the sports-minded Theodore Roosevelt (who personally did not like baseball). Johnson's choice of the name American League was an inspired one.

When the National League dropped four teams, Cleveland, Baltimore, Louisville, and Washington, after the 1899 season, Johnson saw his chance to upgrade his league. In 1900 he installed teams in Detroit, Cleveland, Chicago, Milwaukee, Minneapolis, Kansas City, and Indianapolis and began to lay the groundwork for a still larger expansion. These teams improved the quality of play by adding players freed when the National League reduced its size. The National League did not protest and even made a deal with Johnson to allow him to install teams in Chicago and Cleveland in return for financial concessions and rights to a couple of American League players. The Chicago team, run by Charles Comiskey, was a first-rate organization with most of its players drawn from the ranks of the National League. In 1900 it was probably superior to half the teams in the National League.

One of Johnson's greatest skills was in tapping the talents of baseball men who were clearly superior to the business types who in the 1890s ran the National League into the ground. Johnson, for example, saw the abilities of Connie Mack, Clark Griffith, and even John McGraw, and used them to launch his new league. McGraw clashed with Johnson and switched back to the National League after helping start the American League. But Mack, Griffith, and Comiskey provided the foundation of the new league and gave it great stability. Griffith ultimately took over the Washington team, and he or his family kept it going for seventy years. Mack ran the Philadelphia Athletics for fifty years. Comiskey guided the White Sox until the 1930s.

In 1900 Johnson's new league performed well both at the box office and on the field. In February 1901, when Johnson demanded recognition as a major league, the National League refused to give him a hearing. That proved a mistake. Johnson told reporters that the National League would come to regret its action because the "American League will be the principal [baseball] organization of the country within a short time."

Renouncing adherence to the National Agreement,

Johnson began rounding up financial backers to challenge the National League in its own cities. With prosperity rapidly returning to the country, he had no problem in finding investors willing to take a flyer on a game that had lost money over the past decade. In Philadelphia, for instance, Ben and Tom Shibe, wealthy sports equipment manufacturers, were brought together with Connie Mack to organize a team named the Athletics to compete against the Phillies.

With the aid of a wealthy Great Lakes coal dealer, Charles Somers, and Charles Comiskey who took over as owner of the White Sox, Johnson strengthened the Chicago franchise. Somers's contacts also helped place a team in Boston. By the opening of the 1901 season Johnson was well positioned to challenge the senior circuit, still plagued by internal disputes.

Johnson now had teams in key Eastern cities—Boston, Philadelphia, Baltimore, and Washington—as well as strong Midwestern sites in St. Louis, Cleveland, Detroit, and Chicago. He was unable to crash the New York area because Andrew Freeman had the political connections to deny him a playing site. But the two leagues were equally balanced in population. National League teams were in cities with a total population of 7.5 million while the new league's cities had a total of 6.9 million.

While these maneuvers were taking place, the players in 1900 formed a new organization, the Protective Association of Professional Base Ball Players, modeled after the Brotherhood of a decade earlier. The players recognized that another war between the leagues might enhance their financial position. They were right. In 1901 Johnson gave the signal for his league to raid National League rosters by offering long-term contracts, higher salaries by an average of $500 a year, and promises not to trade players without their consent. The move was successful. Although the figures vary, one source estimates that of 182 players in the American League during the 1901 season, 111 were former National Leaguers.

More important was the high quality of players who jumped to the American League. They included such future Hall of Famers as Napoleon Lajoie, Clark Griffith, Cy Young, John McGraw, and Jimmy Collins. Collins's move demonstrated how well bankrolled the new circuit was. To get him Boston paid a salary of $4,000 plus a $3,500 bonus and 10 percent of the team's profits over $25,000. Collins justified his actions on terms that baseball owners should have understood: "I like to play baseball, but this is a business with me. I can't be governed by sentiment."

The new league even did well at the box office. In its first season of head-to-head rivalry, it drew 1,684,000 fans versus 1,920,000 for the senior circuit. The 3.6 million total gate showed that baseball had fully recovered from the slump of the 1890s with its 1894 low of 1,850,000.

The National League regarded Johnson's challenge the same way it did its earlier conflicts with the American Association and the Players League. It was a problem but not an insurmountable one. In some cases National League owners matched salaries offered by the new league; at other times they turned to the courts to enforce existing contracts.

John Rogers, who owned 51 percent of the Phillies, was outraged when Johnson lured away five of his key players, including such stars as Napoleon Lajoie, Ed Delahanty, and Elmer Flick. Lajoie had signed a three-year contract for $2,400 after the 1900 season. Connie Mack offered him $600 more to play with the Philadelphia Athletics. Rogers refused to match that figure. What made Lajoie even more determined to jump leagues was discovering that the Phillies were paying Delahanty $3,000.

After the 1901 season the hard-hitting (and hard-drinking) Delahanty also quit the Phillies, jumping to Washington
of the American League for a salary of $4,000. Delahanty went
on to lead the new league in 1902 in batting, slugging percentage, and doubles. Rogers had lost the batting champion of the
American League for two consecutive seasons: Lajoie who hit
an astronomical .422 in 1901, and Delahanty whose average
was .376 in 1902. No wonder Rogers was angry, though he had
only himself to blame. For an extra $500 to $600 each he had
lost two of the best hitters in baseball.

Rogers brought suit in Philadelphia, accusing Lajoie of
breach of contract and seeking an injunction to stop him from
playing in the American League. Some of his fellow National
League owners were skeptical of resorting to law because they
didn't want the courts looking too closely at major league
baseball's contractual arrangements. Rogers lost his case
when the court ruled that the standard baseball contract
lacked mutuality: the player's responsibilities were spelled
out while those of the team were not clear. Rogers appealed,
and the Pennsylvania Supreme Court granted him an injunction to prevent Lajoie from playing in Philadelphia. But that
proved valueless when Mack traded Lajoie and Flick to Cleveland after the 1901 season. They would simply not play the
eleven games when Cleveland visited Philadelphia.

The National League was thwarted. They continued to
lose players but were reluctant to seek injunction relief and
allow the courts into the baseball business. In particular they
feared opening up the issue of monopoly, which would bring
baseball under the umbrella of the Sherman Anti-Trust Act.

The 1902 season was a disaster for the National League.
The new league had an exciting pennant race won by Mack's
Philadelphia team by a margin of just 5 games. The top four
teams in the league were separated by a mere 14 games. In

contrast, Pittsburgh won the National League title by 27½ games over second-place Brooklyn. Attendance figures shocked the National League owners. The new circuit outdrew the senior league by more than 220,000 fans. While the American League increased its attendance over the 1901 season, the National League saw its figure drop by 237,000. The Philadelphia Athletics outdrew the New York Giants, the most successful National League team, by 140,000 fans and topped the Phillies by 300,000. The American League was here to stay.

## *Peace Comes to Baseball*

SOMETIME AFTER the 1902 season Ban Johnson was dining out in New York when he was approached by a contingent of National League owners to discuss an end to the baseball dispute. Peace talks soon began between the two leagues. It was clear that the American League had established parity with the senior circuit and that continued fighting would only benefit the players by increasing salaries.

The terms worked out in a matter of days were to last major league baseball for half a century. The two leagues settled all their differences and agreed to "co-exist peacefully and to abstain from signing the other league's players." Each league would respect the other's rights, the reserve clause would be restored, and territories were defined. Both leagues were to share New York, Boston, Chicago, Philadelphia, and St. Louis. The National League was to have special rights in Cincinnati and Pittsburgh while the junior circuit was awarded Washington, Detroit, and Cleveland.

A new National Commission was established, composed of the president of each league plus a third member chosen by the other two. The president of the National League, Harry

Pulliam, was a former newspaperman from Louisville who had entered baseball as an aide to Barney Dreyfuss, the owner of the Pirates. Pulliam was hard-working, conscientious, overly sensitive, and no match for Johnson, his American League counterpart. The chairman of the Commission, chosen by Pulliam and Johnson, was Garry Herrmann, the president of the Cincinnati Reds. Herrmann was part of a powerful Ohio political machine and a longtime baseball man. Good-natured and liked by most baseball people, he too was dominated by Johnson. By his energy, intelligence, and clear sense of direction, Johnson led the Commission throughout its history until he was replaced in 1920 by Judge Kenesaw Mountain Landis.

The Commission effectively administered baseball through the traumatic period when the sport reestablished its hold over the American public. It guided the game away from the frenetic franchise shifts and player jumping that had plagued it for more than twenty years. Stability became a feature of the major leagues, with no franchise changes for fifty years.

Under Johnson, the Commission was determined to provide baseball with a positive image. Umpire baiting, which had been one of the banes of the game, was reduced, though John McGraw periodically caused trouble. When necessary the Commission cracked down and backed the umpires, a step that sent the message that baseball was a fair and honest sport.

Some problems persisted, in particular gambling and alcoholism. Ed Delahanty, one of the greatest hitters of his era, died as a result of his drinking. A functioning alcoholic, Delahanty often was out of control. While playing for Washington in July 1903 his drinking forced him to leave the team while in Detroit and board a train for New York. While the details are not fully clear, he apparently caused such an uproar on the

train that the conductor had him put off at the Canadian end
of the bridge over the Niagara River. Delahanty apparently
tried to walk across the bridge and somehow fell into the river.
His body washed up a couple of days later. It is difficult to estimate the extent of baseball's problem with alcoholism in the
first decades of the new century. It may have been less than in
the 1880s and 1890s, but there is enough anecdotal evidence
to conclude that alcohol was still the drug of choice for baseball players right down to the 1960s.

Johnson was determined to provide a gambling-free
game and remove fans' doubts about the honesty of the contest. He wanted to sever the connection between baseball and
betting that had plagued the sport in the 1880s and 1890s. It
was a difficult task, for gambling parlors specializing in sports
betting could be found throughout the country, especially in
the big cities. Many betting parlors were found in the pool
halls and saloons that baseball players frequented, always a
dangerous sign. Spalding warned his fellow owners that elimi-
nation of betting "was the cornerstone of the success of base
ball." That proved difficult to accomplish, as the Black Sox
scandal would later demonstrate.

One of the new Commission's first decisions was to revive
the championship playoff. After the 1903 season a best-
of-nine series was arranged between the National League–
winning Pirates and the American League champions, the
Boston Pilgrims or Puritans.

Both were good teams. Owners hoped that the playoff—
called with typical baseball exaggeration the World Series—
would deepen interest in the sport. Pittsburgh, led by its star
shortstop and batting champion Honus Wagner, hard-hitting
third baseman Tommy Leach, and outfielder Fred Clarke, was
regarded as clearly the better team.

A powerful, ungainly-looking man with huge hands and

bowed legs, Wagner was amazingly graceful in the field. He undoubtedly was the greatest player of his era. Playing a key position, shortstop, he attained a lifetime batting average of .329 and won eight batting titles. John McGraw, no mean judge of baseball skills, once said of Wagner that he was the nearest approach to baseball perfection he had ever seen.

Boston had just two .300 hitters but a first-class pitching staff led by thirty-six-year-old Cy Young, who won twenty-eight games, and Bill Dinneen, who won twenty. Pittsburgh was the clear favorite but lost to Boston 5 games to 3, a loss that further signaled the maturity of the new league. Wagner had a poor series, hitting just .222, but it was Boston's pitching with a series ERA of 2.03 that won for the Pilgrims.

The series was a popular success with the fans and a financial benefit to the players. The winning players' share was $1,182 each while the losing Pirates actually received $134 more because their owner, Barney Dreyfuss, threw his share to the players. Still, the World Series money was approximately half of the player's regular salary. Not bad for two weeks' work.

The World Series was a financial success for the owners too. Gross receipts were only $50,000 in 1903, but they doubled by 1906 and in 1912 reached $490,000, with the winning player's share reaching $4,000 and the loser's $2,600.

In 1904 the Giants won the National League title while Boston repeated in the American League. But the Giants' owners, Brush and McGraw, refused to play in the World Series: they didn't wish to do anything that might help the new league. "There is nothing in the constitution or playing rules of the National League which requires its victorious club to submit its championship honors to a contest with a victorious club in a minor league," was Brush's way of rejecting postseason play. McGraw was happy to spite Johnson, who had driven him out of the American League a few years before. "Ban Johnson," he said "has not been on the level with me personally and the American League management has been crooked more than once." Johnson stewed, but there was nothing he could do. Fans and sportswriters complained bitterly, accusing Brush and McGraw of pettiness, malice, cowardice, and a "baby act." The Giants players were also unhappy because it cost them money.

During the next season the pressure for a playoff format from fans and sportswriters overcame Brush and McGraw's opposition. Brush even drew up the procedures for World Series play which remained more or less unchanged until the emergence of divisional play in 1969. Brush's plan called for the Series to be decided in the best of seven games, not best of nine.

In 1905 the Giants won again, but in the American League Connie Mack's Athletics beat out Chicago by 2 games with Boston falling to fourth place. The World Series of 1905 was both an artistic and financial success between two excellent teams led by men who personified distinct but equally successful approaches to baseball. McGraw was the aggressive, hard-driving, win-at-all-cost manager who specialized in the "inside" game popular at the time. His Giants in 1905 led the National League with 291 stolen bases, 102 more than the A's.

Mack was a first-class baseball mind with a more gentle approach to handling his players. His team hit 18 points less than the Giants, but his pitching staff included three 20-game winners. Mack was often quoted as saying that baseball was 75 percent pitching, and his 1905 team demonstrated that. Its ERA was 2.19.

Curiously, the A's were beaten in the Series by good pitching, 4 games to 1. Part of the explanation for the A's defeat was the loss of their great lefthander Rube Waddell, who had led the American League in wins, ERA, and strikeouts. Some idea of Waddell's speed can be discerned from the fact that he struck out ten or more batters sixty times in his career, and this at a time when players did not swing hard but rather tried to put the ball in play. Waddell hurt his arm horsing around, trying to destroy a teammate's straw hat, and couldn't pitch in the Series. Rumors, never substantiated, suggested that Waddell had been bribed by gamblers.

Every game of the 1905 Series was a shutout, with the great Christy Mathewson hurling three and "Iron Man" Joe McGinnity the other. Chief Bender, the Chippewa Indian from Carlisle College, won the only game for the A's when he beat the Giants 3 to 0 in game two.

After 1905 the World Series was a fixture as the capstone of the baseball season. Within a short time the new league asserted its superiority. The White Sox team of 1906, the famous "hitless wonders," a squad which hit just 7 home runs all season and batted .230, defeated a crosstown rival that on paper was one of the greatest teams of all time. The 1906 Cubs won 116 games, the most in baseball history. Five of their pitchers had ERAs under 2.00, with one, Mordecai "Three Finger" Brown, so-called because he had maimed his fingers while working on farm machinery, winning 26 games with an incredible ERA of 1.04. On the field the Cubs were led by the double-play combination made famous by the New York columnist Franklin P. Adams's doggerel, "Tinker to Evers to Chance." (Interestingly, this most-heralded double-play combination in history was not even the best in the National League in 1906. Two teams made more double plays that season, and none of the Cubs threesome led the league in double plays at his position.)

Over the next three years the National League reasserted

its dominance in the fall classic over the American League champion Tigers led by the young Ty Cobb. The Cubs won in 1907 and 1908; the Pirates, led by Wagner who outplayed Cobb, won in 1909. From that point, however, the American League swept five of the next six Series, with Connie Mack's A's winning three world championships.

Clearly the two leagues were now roughly equal and the talent evenly spread. One apparent difference had to do with the background of the players in each league. The National League remained dominated by players of Irish and German heritage who came mostly from the cities of the North and East. The American League drew more from the Midwest. Cobb, who first made it to the majors in 1905, was the forerunner of the Southern country boys who would enter baseball in the 1920s and 1930s. The junior circuit also attracted a surprising number of college men to its ranks, perhaps influenced by Johnson's determination to play a cleaner brand of baseball. One authority has estimated that 25 percent of the players in the majors in 1910 had attended college compared with less than 5 percent for men of their age outside of baseball.

A close examination of the two leagues in the first decade of the twentieth century shows that the American League developed better talent. Among future Hall of Famers who began playing in the American League between 1901 and 1910 were Cobb, Tris Speaker, Walter Johnson, Harry Hooper, Eddie Collins, Chief Bender, Eddie Plank, and Home Run Baker. The senior circuit could not boast of such an impressive list.

Connie Mack in particular had a fondness for college types, perhaps because of his dealings with the unruly Waddell. Mack's best pitchers in the first years of the century were college men: Eddie Plank of Gettysburg, Jack Coombs of

Colby, and Chief Bender of Carlisle. Mack also signed future
Hall of Famer Eddie Collins in 1906 fresh off the college campus. College types came to see that baseball not only paid
salaries commensurate with respectable occupations such as
doctors and lawyers but also conveyed enormous prestige and
fame. Many players would use their major league experience
to secure jobs as college coaches when their careers ended.

By the end of the first decade of the new century, baseball had not only returned to its position as American's National Game, it had also become respectable. It was now one
of the very measures of what constituted being American.

*The early Ebbets Field in Brooklyn.*

# Chapter 4

# THE WARS
# OF BASEBALL,
# 1909–1918

AT THE BEGINNING of the second decade of the twentieth century baseball was thriving. On the surface it
seemed to have solved most of its pressing problems. Attendance was booming, interleague conflicts were diminishing,
and a new generation of talented players indicated that baseball remained the first choice of talented male athletes.

From the formation of the American League in 1901,
baseball attendance had risen every year until in 1909 it
reached 7,236,000. For the first decade of the new century,
major league baseball had attracted just under 50 million
fans, an impressive figure for a sport that had gone through
serious economic difficulties just a few years before. Baseball's success mirrored the rapid growth of American cities
early in the century. The game that had become an urban phenomenon early in its history now became a source of pride to
the cities that held a major league franchise.

Fans flocked to games, taking advantage of the new trolley lines that opened up all parts of the city to cheap, fast transportation. Ballparks were located along the routes where trolley lines met. When it opened in 1913, for example, Ebbets Field was at the conjunction of nine trolley lines. This type of siting was typical of the wave of baseball parks constructed between 1909 and 1916. It appears that most of fans used public transportation to get to the games. The automobile was in its infancy and used only by better-off fans. Shibe Park, when it opened in 1909, featured a two-hundred-car public garage with a full service department located under the right-field wall. Old photographs taken around 1910 show rows of parked cars near the ballpark. But it was still a luxury.

While it is difficult to pinpoint the social class of the fans at this time, it appears that the game drew chiefly from the middle class and the upper ranks of the working class—people with enough money to afford a ticket and the time off to attend a game. Weekday games usually attracted the more affluent fan while on weekends the stands were filled with blue-collar types. Ticket prices remained reasonable: $1 to $1.25 for covered grandstand; 50 cents for bleachers. Ban Johnson's determination to attract a better quality of fan apparently worked, but there were enough working-class types to give the game a democratic look in the first years of the century. The Boston Pilgrims of the American League, for example, had a loyal Irish working-class rooting section led by a saloonkeeper, "Nuf Ced" McGreevy. Other teams had similar followings. Again photographs show that the fans were overwhelmingly male, wearing derbies or cloth caps, sure signs of lower-middle-class to working-class respectability. Yet the most famous song in all sports history, "Take Me Out to the Ball-Game," was written by Jack Norworth in 1908 about a girl asking her beau to take her to a game. Baseball, however, for years remained virtually oblivious to the possibility of attracting women fans, a sign of the lack of imagination and hidebound nature of those who ran the sport.

Other than growing attendance figures, there were a number of clear indications that professional baseball was prospering. The cost of a major league franchise rose rapidly throughout the first years of the century. The Boston National League team was sold for $75,000 in 1906 but five years later commanded $187,000. The Chicago Cubs sold for $105,000 in 1905 and $500,000 in 1915. McGraw's Giants, one of the most successful clubs in baseball, were sold for $125,000 in 1903, a great sum in those days. Sixteen years later the Wall Street broker Charles Stoneham paid $1,820,000 for the team. There was no lack of buyers as sportsmen and business types saw great commercial possibilities in baseball as well as a way of showing that they were civic benefactors.

Another sign of prosperity was the building of new ballparks. From 1909 to 1914, ten ballparks were built or renovated with modern construction techniques. The old wooden park, always a fire hazard, thrown up in a matter of days or weeks for a few thousand dollars, gave way to a series of modern ballparks of which two still survive at this writing: Wrigley Field in Chicago and Fenway Park in Boston.

In 1909 Benjamin Franklin Shibe undertook the construction of a new steel and concrete ballpark in Philadelphia which would overshadow anything in the game and make the "City of Brotherly Love" the envy of the baseball world. He bought land at 21st and Lehigh Avenue in a rapidly developing part of north Philadelphia with easy access by train and trolley. The land cost $67,000 and the ballpark itself $301,000. Shibe wanted not only a fine ballpark but "a lasting monument" that would express the progressive views of the age.

He got what he wanted. Shibe Park, as it came to be called, was a modern structure which featured an ornate façade in French Renaissance style. It had a covered grand-stand which seated eight thousand while another twelve thousand seats were provided in uncovered bleachers that ran from first and third bases to the outfield walls. When the park opened in April 1909 police estimated that thirty thousand fans attended, with the crowd arriving as early as seven in the morning.

Four months later Barney Dreyfuss of Pittsburgh, never afraid to spend money, opened his new modern park in the Oakland–Schenley Park section of the city. His structure was even more opulent than Shibe Park. Costing $2 million and comfortably seating 25,000 fans, it had a triple-decked grandstand and was equipped with elevators and telephones. Dreyfuss took a chance by locating his new ballpark far from downtown Pittsburgh. He had the advice of Andrew Carnegie, who recommended the location as worth the risk. "There was nothing there but a livery stable and a hothouse," Dreyfuss recalled years later, "with a few cows grazing over the countryside." Dreyfuss won a $150 bet from a friend that he would never be able to fill the faraway ballpark. He noted that the opening of the park, named Forbes Field after a British general of the French and Indian War, drew 30,000 fans. It was filled to capacity five times in the first two weeks after it opened.

Not to be outdone, the next year Charles Comiskey commissioned a modern structure for his Chicago White Stockings. Construction of Comiskey Park, as it was eventually known, began appropriately enough on St. Patrick's Day 1910 and was completed in less than five months at a cost of $750,000. Modeled on the Roman Coliseum, it seated 28,000 fans with no difficulty.

Shibe Park, Forbes Field, and Comiskey Park were architectural marvels with wide comfortable seats, covered grandstands, and plush clubhouses for the players. These "green cathedrals," as they came to be known, set the style for baseball parks for the next fifty years. Within a few years every team in the major leagues, except the Phillies, had either built a new park or completely remodeled an older field along the lines of Shibe Park, Forbes Field, and Comiskey Park. There was a no clearer sign of baseball prosperity than this massive building program, at an average cost of $500,000 to $1 million, which combined modern building techniques with a willingness on the part of the baseball establishment to invest money in order to make money.

The rush to build new playing fields for baseball was an indication that the sport had escaped from its image as a rough, rowdy game and begun the transformation into big business. Men who invested $750,000 to $2 million in a baseball franchise had a deep stake in the community. The likelihood of them pulling up stakes, moving to a new city, or jumping leagues diminished as the financial depth of their commitment grew. The teams and their owners formed close working relations with the political elite in their cities, and this partnership benefited baseball for almost a half-century. By 1910 the stability that baseball had achieved reinforced its claim to be America's national game.

## The A's and Giants Dynasties

A SURE SIGN of baseball's growing significance as a cultural icon was the appearance of President William Howard Taft to throw out the ceremonial first ball of the 1910 season. As a young man Taft had wanted to play professional baseball, but his mother didn't approve of his associating with the roughnecks who dominated the sport. It soon became expected that the president continue the tradition established by the baseball-loving Taft. In 1915 Woodrow Wilson became the first president to attend a World Series game when he went to Philadelphia to watch the Phillies and Red Sox play.

Another sign of the health of the game was its high caliber of play. By 1910 the new playing talent had matured and would dominate the game for a decade. Cobb, Speaker, Walter Johnson, Grover Cleveland Alexander, the young Joe Jackson who came into his own in 1911 by hitting .400—all peaked in the second decade of the century. In Cobb, baseball produced its first true superstar. The fiery Georgian was a perfectionist who in his own words had to "be first all the time."

Cobb personified the best and worst of baseball in the so-called Dead Ball era. A left-handed batter, he held the bat with his hands apart so that could either "choke up" and slap at the pitch or slide his hands to the end and swing hard. Cobb set offensive records that lasted for seven decades. He was the first player to achieve 4,000 hits. His 96 stolen bases in one season stood until 1962. Cobb won an unmatched 12 batting titles, including 9 in a row, and hit better than .400 three times. He still holds the record for most runs scored in a career, 2,245, and the highest lifetime batting average, .367.

As a player, Cobb's drive to succeed often alienated his teammates and managers. "Wahoo Sam" Crawford, a fine Hall of Fame outfielder who played alongside Cobb, found him to be a despicable human being, a racist, and a bully. With it all, Cobb was one of baseball's first great drawing cards. Fans loved to watch him.

New and better equipment, especially improved gloves, elevated the quality of play and especially aided the defense. Total errors in the American League dropped almost 20 percent between 1901 and 1910. The introduction of shin guards in 1907 by the catcher Roger Bresnahan, though greeted with derision by fans and players alike, was soon accepted throughout baseball. It enabled the catcher to move closer to the batter, thus improving his chances of throwing out base-stealers, and it made it easier for him to block the plate on close plays.

Between 1910 and 1914 major league baseball was dominated by two excellent teams, Connie Mack's revived A's and John McGraw's Giants. Both teams had dominated the early years of the century but had fallen behind. By 1909 Mack and McGraw had revamped their teams, in the process showing how to revive a franchise. Beginning in 1909 Mack built a new A's pennant contender around a combination of superb pitching and solid if unspectacular hitting and defense. The 1909 A's won 95 games, finishing 3 games behind Cobb's last pennant-winning Tigers team. Four of Mack's pitchers, Eddie Plank, Chief Bender, Cy Morgan, and Harry Krause, had ERAs under 2.00. The pennant-winning A's team of 1910 had a team ERA of 1.79. Eddie Collins at second and Frank Baker (soon to be nicknamed "Home Run") at third were future Hall of Famers. The A's team of these years was known for its "$100,000 Infield" because of the high quality of the players. Stuffy McInnis, the team's first baseman, was a lifetime .300 hitter while shortstop Jack Barry was a weak hitter but a fine defensive player for his time. The A's outfield was mediocre compared to the pitching staff and infield.

Mack's squad included four future Hall of Famers: Bender, Plank, Baker, and Collins. In some ways the 1910–1914 A's were Mack's best team because they won three World Series.

McGraw's Giants won 92 games in 1909 and 91 in 1910 but finished behind the great Pirates and Cubs teams. The Cubs won over 100 games in 1909 and 1910. McGraw built his team around the pitching of Christy Mathewson and a solid hitting squad led by such fine if not spectacular players as Fred Merkle at first, Josh Devore in the outfield, and Chief Meyers behind the plate. Like all players with Indian blood, Meyers was called "Chief," a perfect reflection of the naiveté and racism of the age. Meyers was easily the best defensive catcher in the National League as well as a decent hitter. He was responsible for handling the pitching the way McGraw wanted: keep the score close, and the Giants with speed and good hitting would win the game. McGraw's team typically either led the league in stolen bases or was among the top three during these years. For example, the pennant-winning Giants of 1911 stole 347 bases, 57 more than their nearest competitor.

The 1909–1914 Giants and A's were among the best in baseball history. Fans responded: both teams led their leagues in attendance in four of the six years between 1909 and 1914.

Mack's A's gained revenge for losing the 1905 World Series to the Giants by beating them in 1911 and 1913. These victories were particularly sweet for Mack, for McGraw had consistently ridiculed the A's as Mack's "White Elephants." It was during the 1911 World Series that Frank Baker won back-to-back games by hitting clutch late-inning homers, winning him enduring fame as "Home Run" Baker. Baker was, in fact, a long-ball threat, winning the home run title four years in a row, 1911–1914, a feat that only Babe Ruth and Ralph Kiner have duplicated in baseball history.

Despite the fine play of the A's and Giants, something was disturbing baseball. Attendance in the major leagues began a decline in 1909 that, given the quality of play and the opening of new baseball palaces, made no sense. Between 1909 and 1913 attendance dropped almost 900,000. No satisfactory explanation has been offered. True, the pennant races in both leagues during this time were not competitive. But even the

A's team that won the pennant in 1913 drew 100,000 fewer fans than the third-place team of 1909. Mack came to believe that fans liked to see a team develop as a contender rather than come out to see a successful team win.

When baseball's leadership awoke to the problem of declining attendance, it thrashed about for a realistic answer. *Reach's Guide* for 1915 put the blame squarely on external factors. "Political unrest and revolution in the nation . . . the constant harassment and depression of the country's big and little businesses . . . the competition of such cheap daytime amusements as the 'movies'"—all were cited as contributing to baseball's troubles. But this is hardly satisfactory. Political unrest in the country in these years was no match for the populism of the mid-1890s. By no stretch of the imagination could one describe the United States as "revolutionary" between 1910 and 1915. William Howard Taft and Woodrow Wilson scarcely qualify as overthrowers of the Establishment.

The American economy, however, was struggling during these years. Per capita income actually fell between 1909 and 1915, from $1,290 to $1,238. Unemployment, at 8.1 percent in 1908, dropped briefly and then rose sharply until it reached a post-1890s depression high of 8.9 percent. A brief but severe recession occurred in mid-1914 as the United States adjusted to the outbreak of war in Europe.

The real villain of baseball's problems in mid-decade was simpler to understand. In 1914 major league baseball was challenged by a new league, the Federal, at a time when the baseball establishment thought it had beaten back the threat of rival leagues once and for all.

## The Federal League War

DESPITE AN ATTENDANCE DECLINE in the early teens, the profitability of major league baseball continued to attract investors who were on the prowl for new and lucrative enterprises. It was clear that big money could be made in baseball. The Cubs earned $1.2 million between 1906 and 1915 while the Giants' profit was $100,000 each year from 1906 to 1910. According to records published during one of Congress's many investigations of baseball, the gross operating income of the major leagues in the first half of the second decade of the century topped $20 million. This was big money by any standards and particularly attractive in light of the way the American League had gained acceptance as a major league in just a few years. Major league baseball sought to discourage raiders by not publishing attendance figures for each league. But this ploy didn't work because newspapers provided good estimates of yearly attendance.

In November 1913 a group of businessmen led by James Gilmore, a wealthy Chicago stationer, set out to organize a new league that they named the Federal League. Initially major league baseball viewed this as just another minor league. But Gilmore had bigger plans. His group included successful businessmen such as Charles Weeghman, who owned a chain of Chicago lunchrooms; Otto Steifel, a St. Louis brewer; St. Louis icehouse owner Philip de Catesby Ball; the Ward brothers of New York, who owned the successful Tip Top Bakery; and Harry Sinclair, a phenomenally rich oilman who would later gain notoriety in the Teapot Dome scandal during the Harding administration. Like most baseball owners, these men, with the exception of Sinclair, were of recent ethnic stock. They were aggressive, successful capitalists, classic examples of the types Woodrow Wilson characterized admiringly as "men on the make."

These owners ensured that the Federal League would not be short of cash. They expected within a couple of years to duplicate the success of the American League by gaining major league status. In theory their optimism was justified. But when Ban Johnson had challenged the National League monopoly fifteen years earlier, he had started from a stronger position. He had carefully built up the American League and launched his challenge when the National League was weakened by internal rivalries. And the country was just recovering from economic hard times. Gilmore and his associates were challenging baseball at a time of solid success, even if attendance had slipped.

Major league baseball expected the Federal League to fold as other leagues had. But Gilmore's group was well financed and in 1914 demanded recognition as a major league. The National Commission adamantly refused. Ban Johnson told Gilmore that "there was not room for three major leagues." Gilmore refused to back off. That year, 1914, Federal League teams were established in Baltimore, Brooklyn, Buffalo, Chicago, Kansas City, Pittsburgh, St. Louis, and Indianapolis. These choices highlight the new league's problems. Three of the cities, Buffalo, Baltimore, and Indianapolis, were classic minor league towns where major league baseball had failed in the recent past. More important, the Federal League had failed to establish teams in the biggest cities of the East, New York and Philadelphia. The new league promptly began raiding the majors, declaring that they did not recognize the National Agreement nor would they respect the reserve clause. That meant war.

In 1914–1915 major league owners had no desire to share

their profits with newcomers. Johnson found himself in an embarrassing position, for the Federal League was simply duplicating what he had successfully attempted fifteen years earlier. But he refused to give an inch.

The struggle proved disastrous for baseball at all levels. In a short time the Federals had lured away some of the best talent of the National and American leagues. Joe Tinker was the first celebrated player to jump—he signed a three-year, $36,000 contract with the Chicago team of the Federal League. Thus the two existing Chicago teams would face a rival led by a local hero. Three Finger Brown also was an early jumper: he was hired as playing manager by the St. Louis team of the Federal League. In all, eighty-one major leaguers joined the Federal League, including such future Hall of Famers as Tinker, Brown, Eddie Plank, Chief Bender, and Edd Roush. The Federal League treated players more fairly than did the existing majors. The reserve clause of the Federal contract was modified so as to give the players more freedom, and raises of 5 percent a year were guaranteed.

These signings created a crisis for the major leagues. For one thing, they raised salaries to all-time high levels just at a time when baseball players were showing an interest in organizing again as they had in the 1880s. In 1912 a New York lawyer and former player, Dave Fultz, chartered a new organization called the Base Ball Players Fraternity. (The Players Protective Association had died in 1903 when the two leagues made peace.) Within a few months he had enrolled three hundred players, and eventually the membership reached twelve hundred. Fultz pressed the major leagues for concessions to players on issues such as respect for all contracts, protection from abusive fans, and help with financial and career advice.

At first Fultz was palmed off with a few crumbs, but with the emergence of the third league clamoring for players, he became a serious threat. Fortunately for the baseball owners, Fultz was a moderate who tried to improve the lot of his members without harming professional baseball. He was cautious as a result of past unsuccessful attempts to organize players. He also understood that the public preferred an "open shop" and was unsympathetic toward unions in general. He didn't want to alienate the owners if he could gain concessions without provocation.

As a direct result of Federal League competition, baseball salaries doubled between 1913 and 1915, from an average $3,200 to $7,300. (At the time blue-collar workers earned $700 a year and skilled craftsmen $1,200.) Ty Cobb's salary doubled to $20,000; Walter "Rabbit" Maranville, then a young shortstop, saw his pay rise from $1,800 to $6,000; Walter Johnson, the American League's premier pitcher, simply by flirting with the Federal League team in Chicago, got a raise from $7,000 to $12,500 plus a $6,000 bonus for staying with the Washington Senators. The payrolls of major league teams that had averaged $51,000 before the Federal League now rose to more than $70,000 within two years.

After fifteen flush years, major league baseball could see red ink ahead. Attendance plummeted as fans were disgusted by players jumping from league to league. In 1914 the National League drew just 1.7 million fans, its lowest figure since the emergence of the two leagues in 1903 and below some of the depression years of the 1890s. Cincinnati, for example, drew slightly more than 100,000 fans for the entire 1914 season while the Phillies' attendance plummeted by 300,000 for the year. The *New York Times* estimated that half the teams in baseball lost money in 1914; those that finished in the black showed only marginal profits.

The Philadelphia A's, while winning their fourth pennant in five years, drew 225,000 fewer fans than in 1913 and the

smallest number of any American League pennant winner
since 1907. Mack was ready to break up his dynasty even before his vaunted A's team was swept in the World Series by the
"Miracle Braves," so named because Boston came from last
place in July to win the National League pennant. The 1914
World Series was the first time a losing team had failed to win
at least one game. Mack was mortified. He had lost $60,000 in
1914 despite taking his team to the World Series.

He now decided to break up the A's before losing his players to the Federal League. Shortly after the World Series he
began a fire sale. Mack believed that some of his veterans were
over the hill and not worth the huge salaries they would command due to competition from the Federal League. He eventually lost Bender, Plank, Barry, Baker, and Eddie Collins but
recouped $180,000 for them.

In the Federal League's second year, 1915, attendance for
the two established leagues increased slightly, but the total
was still smaller than in 1903. A dozen years of economic
progress had been wiped out; all three leagues were in debt
with no end in sight. Federal League losses for 1915 were put
at $2.5 million, a figure even the millionaires who owned these
teams couldn't bear for long. The Ward brothers, who owned
Brooklyn, absorbed losses of more than $800,000; the Federal
League franchises in Kansas City and Buffalo were broke.

Tentative peace talks opened in April 1915 but then collapsed. As early as May, Gilmore knew that the Federal
League was doomed. In July he admitted that the new league
was "fighting a hopeless task. There were two clubs that had
practically given up the fight, Kansas City and Buffalo." He
didn't believe that the league could continue with six clubs.

Gilmore decided on an audacious plan. Along with Sinclair and one of the Ward brothers, R. B., he leaked the details
of a plan to invade New York for the 1916 season. He hoped to

scare the majors into cutting a deal by threatening one of their most important centers. Gilmore later admitted that the threat was nothing but "one big bluff," designed to compel baseball to buy out the Federal League. It worked.

The Federal League went forward in the fall of 1915 as if it was seriously planning for a new season. In December 1915 Gilmore bumped into three members of the National League in a New York City hotel. He was asked to sit down and discuss common problems, but he refused. Gilmore told the three National League representatives that the Federal League had no interest in peace talks.

The next day he was approached again, and with Harry Sinclair in tow Gilmore began serious discussions for a settlement. The final terms were worked out quickly.

The Federal League would disband. Players under contract to Federal League teams would be sold to the major leagues for a nice profit. The National League offered $400,000 for the Brooklyn Federal franchise as a sign of goodwill. They also bought out the Pittsburgh Federals, but for only $50,000. Charles Weeghman was given an opportunity to buy the Cubs. He moved them into his new ballpark that later became known as Wrigley Field. Phil Ball, another powerful Federal owner, bought the St. Louis Cardinals team that had been in financial difficulties for years. Finally it was agreed that there would be no reprisals directed at players who had jumped leagues. Aside from Benny Kauff, winner of two batting titles and known as the Ty Cobb of the Federal League, interest in purchasing the contracts of the jumpers was milder than it had been after other league wars.

The peace treaty was a good deal for everyone; all sides were losing money. According to some estimates, baseball lost more than $10 million in the Federal League war. That figure may be inflated, but surely the game had suffered a loss of interest as the squabbling turned fans to indifference just as baseball's popularity was growing.

Federal League officials with power and influence were bought out; a couple of owners entered the inner circle of professional baseball; and playing talent was redistributed around the major leagues. Peace lasted for thirty years until the threat of the Mexican League after World War II threw a scare into major league baseball. Businessmen learned that even a prosperous sport like baseball was a costly venture to try to crash. Even in the lucrative 1920s, baseball's so-called "Golden Age," there was no interest in creating a rival league. The Federal League squabble doomed that kind of thinking.

Baltimore was the only team to suffer a real loss. Its owners had been misled by Gilmore and Sinclair, first into believing that the Federal League would continue in 1916, then into expecting a franchise in the majors. But the major league owners rejected Baltimore out of hand. The city had failed to support a major league franchise early in the century and was considered not deserving a second chance. Baltimore was, in the words of Charles Ebbets of the Dodgers, "one of the worst minor towns" in America. Besides, Ebbets noted in a remark typical of the racially insensitive times, Baltimore had "too many colored population to start with. They are a cheap population when it gets down to paying their money at the gate."

Baltimore's owners sued the major leagues in a landmark anti-trust case that went all the way to the Supreme Court where professional baseball won an exemption from anti-trust legislation. Initially the Supreme Court of the District of Columbia found for Baltimore, awarding the owners triple damages of $240,000 under the terms of the Sherman Anti-Trust Act. This decision was reversed by the D.C. Court of Appeals. The case then began working its way up to the United States

Supreme Court where in 1922 it established baseball's unique position in law.

## *"Work or Fight"*

NO SOONER had the Federal League mess been cleared away than baseball entered another period of crisis, this time associated with a real war, World War I, and then with the scandal that nearly destroyed the game.

In 1916 baseball bounced back from the Federal League war as attendance rose by 33 percent. Close pennant races in both leagues were largely responsible for this boomlet. The Red Sox, let by a young, rawboned lefthander named George Herman "Babe" Ruth who won 23 games, edged out a solid White Sox club by 2 games. In the National League, Brooklyn won its first title since 1899 by an equally slim margin of 2½ games as the Robins (named after their rotund manager, "Uncle" Wilbert Robinson) beat out the Phillies who looked to repeat. The World Series, however, was a letdown as the Red Sox swept four of five games. While the games were close, none was particularly exciting except for game two which Ruth won by going 14 innings and giving up just 1 run.

Even with peace restored, attendance overall was still less than the majors had attracted eight years earlier. With competition stifled, major league owners began to reduce salaries to pre–Federal League levels. Honus Wagner had to accept a cut of more than 40 percent, from $10,000 to $5,400, while the Red Sox trimmed Tris Speaker from $18,000 to $9,000. Speaker held out and as a result was traded to Cleveland where he eventually was named manager. Fultz's Players Fraternity soon found that it was being frozen out by major league baseball, no longer worried by competition. By 1917 his organization was a dead letter.

Before the 1917 season began, the United States had entered World War I. At first major league baseball believed that it would remain untouched by the conflict, as it had during the Spanish-American War. In order to show their patriotism the league presidents, led by Ban Johnson, directed that men in uniform be admitted to games free and that fans be urged to buy war bonds. Johnson also offered a $500 bonus to the American League team that was best in military drill. The hapless St. Louis Browns, who had never won anything in American League history, won the prize as the best-drilled team in baseball.

Baseball got through the 1917 season relatively undisturbed by the war, though it lost some of its players, among them Hank Gowdy, the talented catcher of the Boston Braves, to the military. Once again, however, attendance dipped sharply to 5.2 million. Excluding the Federal League years, this figure was the lowest the major leagues had attracted since 1903, the first year of the American–National League peace agreement.

The decline in attendance may have been influenced by two noncompetitive pennant races as well as by the distraction of a greater contest, war. McGraw's Giants won by 10 games over the Phillies despite a second straight 30-victory season for Grover Cleveland Alexander. In the American League the White Sox ran away from the rest of the league, beating the Red Sox by 9 games. The World Series lasted six games with the White Sox winning despite Benny Kauff, a refugee from the Federal League, hitting two homers in game four for the Giants, only the second time that feat had been achieved since the beginning of post-season play in 1903. Playing in the two largest ballparks in the majors, the games averaged 31,000 attendance, second highest in World Series history. The players' share of moneys was less than in the preceding year because of wartime taxes.

World War I was something new and different for baseball's buccaneer businessmen. The emotional patriotism, hatred of "the Hun," and denunciation of slackers caught them off guard. The drilling of baseball players, the flying of the American flag, and donations to the Red Cross would not be enough to save major league baseball if the war dragged on for long. Unlike World War II, where a sympathetic President Roosevelt saw a real morale value in continuing baseball for the war's duration, the Wilson administration was led by humorless zealots.

In May 1918, Secretary of War Newton Baker issued an order that essentially called on eligible men to do war work or join the armed services. Eventually 227 major leaguers joined the military, including such stars as Ty Cobb and Christy Mathewson. Mathewson was inadvertently gassed during basic training, leading to complications of lung problems that eventually killed him in 1925.

Baker's order was to go into effect in July. Efforts to secure an exemption for baseball players failed. Johnson, in desperation, recommended canceling the season. A majority of owners overruled him and instead shortened the season to just 140 games. The World Series would be played shortly after Labor Day.

Johnson was angry, but his protests were brushed aside by the owners seeking to salvage the rest of the season. It was the first sign that his unchallenged power was beginning to wane.

The 1918 season ended on a flat note. The World Series played in early September between the Red Sox and Cubs attracted little attention as the American public followed the exploits of United States forces in the final battles of the war. Gate receipts were down, and players received their smallest paychecks in years.

It is doubtful that baseball would have been played in 1919 had the war continued. The minors were barely surviving, and major league owners were ready to close down for the duration when the war came to a sudden end in November 1918. Baseball was saved and the world was safe for democracy, or so the nation believed. Owners and players looked forward to the first postwar campaign with enthusiasm. Baseball was back to normal, and everyone expected to get rich. Instead 1919, which started so promisingly, became one of the black years of baseball history.

*From left, Ty Cobb, Babe Ruth, and Eddie Collins on opening day, 1927, at Yankee Stadium.*

*Chapter 5*

# GOLDEN AGE,
# 1919–1931

T HE YEARS immediately after World War I, until American society stabilized in the early 1920s, were profoundly difficult ones for the nation as well as for the National Game. Postwar readjustment proved painful as the war ended so abruptly, leaving the nation unprepared for peace. Active military personnel peaked in 1918 at 4.7 million, and within a year 1.7 million of them were returned to civilian life. As a result, unemployment, which reached an all-time low of 1.4 percent in 1918 and 1919, slowly began to rise. It was over 5 percent in 1920 and more than double that figure one year later. Per capita income dropped after the war. Labor unrest reached unprecedented levels in 1919 with more than 4 million people on strike at one time or another, including walkouts in steel, coal, the police in Boston, and, most unusually, actors on Broadway.

1919 also saw the first Red Scare, when President Wilson's politically ambitious attorney general, A. Mitchell Palmer, began rounding up anarchists, socialists, and communists suspected of wishing to overthrow the government. This political assault edged into attacks on dissident groups of any kind. Radical violence, always near the surface in American society, spilled out into the open that year as race riots spread throughout the country. An outgrowth of this racial turmoil was the dramatic increase in lynchings of blacks—seventy in 1919, including some in military uniform.

The country seemed out of control as the dislocation of the postwar period took its toll on the nation's frayed nerves. Baseball was able to avoid the worst aspects of this period. The game had barely survived the war, but it had managed to do its patriotic part, thus solidifying its image as America's unique sport.

The 1919 season was a great success considering the concerns of baseball leadership in the final weeks of the 1918 season. In 1919 the schedule was shortened to 140 games, but two good pennant races saw attendance more than double from 1918 and reach 1911 levels. The second-place New York Giants drew 708,000 fans, the highest attendance in the National League since 1909, while the pennant-winning Cincinnati Reds broke their own attendance record by more than 80,000 fans.

In the American League the White Sox on their way to the pennant drew 627,000 fans. The fourth-place Detroit Tigers led the American League in attendance with 640,000 while the rapidly improving Yankees also exceeded 600,000. This was the first time in league history that three teams had bettered 600,000 attendance. It was also a foreshadowing of what would come in the 1920s as major league baseball attendance records were shattered.

The surge in attendance reflected the baseball public's demand for a "return to normalcy" and a desire that the problems of the Federal League and the world war be forgotten. The public seemed to find in baseball a sign of stability in a world plagued by bolshevism, starvation, red scares, and flu pandemics.

While baseball seemed healthy in 1919, a major crisis was in fact brewing. The National Agreement, which had worked so effectively to end the American–National League conflict at the turn of the century and had enabled the game to survive the Federal League squabble, was rapidly unraveling. Some American League owners, led by Colonel Jacob Ruppert of the Yankees, the White Sox's Charles Comiskey, and Harry Frazee of the Red Sox, were angry with Ban Johnson's heavy-handed rule. In the National League some owners were upset with Garry Herrmann, accusing him of being a pawn of Johnson. Barney Dreyfuss, the influential owner of the Pirates, blamed Herrmann and Johnson for denying him the services of the highly touted college player George Sisler. Sisler, destined to be one of the greatest players of the 1920s, had originally agreed to sign with the Pirates but then reneged and in 1915 signed a contract with the St. Louis Browns. Dreyfuss erupted in rage and demanded that he be awarded Sisler, but the three-man executive committee determined that Sisler belonged to the Browns. Dreyfuss never forgave Herrmann and began to enlist other National League owners to oust him as third man on baseball's ruling triumvirate.

Meanwhile Comiskey and Johnson, once close allies, had had a falling out over a number of issues. Johnson's arrogance was getting the best of his judgment, and his imperious style was irritating the hard-nosed business types who owned American League clubs. In 1919, for instance, he tried to void the sale of the talented pitcher Carl Mays from the Red Sox to the Yankees. Ruppert won a court injunction and overcame Johnson's opposition.

Baseball's smooth administration was breaking up. In

1918 John Tener resigned as National League president and was replaced by the more stubborn John Heydler, a former sportswriter, umpire, and statistician for the National League. Herrmann felt increasingly isolated and in 1920 resigned from the National Executive. Johnson, weakened by divisions among American League owners, and Heydler could not agree on a replacement.

The Black Sox scandal erupted in the midst of this administrative turmoil. The 1919 season had been a huge success for baseball. Babe Ruth's emergence as a home run titan had caught the public's attention. Ruth, a superbly talented pitcher for the Red Sox, had shown signs of hitting prowess in the past. He had shared the American League home run title with the A's Tilly Walker during the abbreviated 1918 season—both hit 11 home runs. But in 1919 the Red Sox manager, Ed Barrow, moved Ruth to the outfield. In 138 games he hit the astonishing total of 29 homers, a figure that broke the modern record of 27 set in 1884 by Ned Williamson of Chicago.

In the American League that season, Comiskey had assembled a fine squad of professionals led by second baseman Eddie Collins, right fielder Shoeless Joe Jackson, and twenty-game winners Eddie Cicotte and Lefty Williams. Although divided into bitter factions, the team was held together by the manager, a fine old pitcher, Kid Gleason, as well as the players' hatred of Comiskey, who was notorious for underpaying them. Cicotte, despite winning twenty-nine games for the season, earned $8,000 for the year compared to Cincinnati's highest-paid player, Edd Roush, at $10,000. The White Sox won the pennant by 3½ games over a surging Cleveland team managed by Tris Speaker.

The National League title went to the Cincinnati Reds, who won their first pennant since the organization of the two leagues in 1903. Ably piloted by Pat Moran, the Reds were a

finely balanced team with superb pitching, solid defense, and
average hitting. They had only one good hitter, the National
League batting champ, Edd Roush, plus a solid third baseman in Heinie Groh, famed for using a bat that was shaped
like a bottle. The pitching staff was anchored by Dutch
Ruether, Slim Sallee, and Hod Eller who won 59 and lost 22
for the season. The team ERA of 2.23 helped the Reds easily
defeat McGraw's Giants by 9½ games.

In the mythology of events surrounding the Black Sox
scandal, the White Sox are often portrayed as an infinitely
better team than the Reds, if not one of the greatest in American League history. In fact the White Sox were a talented
squad, but they didn't match up to some of Connie Mack's
great A's teams of the 1910–1915 era, the Ty Cobb–led Tigers
of 1907–1909, or Frank Chance's great Cubs team of the first
decade of the century.

The Reds, on the other hand, were no patsies. They defeated two good clubs, the Giants and the Cubs, on their way
to the pennant and won ninety-eight games (ten more than
the White Sox) in a shortened season. The Reds' winning percentage was the best in the National League in a decade.
Whatever the odds were on the World Series, the Reds were a
talented team that, given a few breaks, could have defeated
the White Sox without help from gamblers.

As the 1919 season wound down, rumors abounded that
the World Series would be fixed. But these kinds of stories had
been around baseball ever since the game became professional
in the 1870s. Some evidence indicates that Comiskey was
warned of trouble and failed to act. When the odds on the
White Sox dropped before game one in Cincinnati, however, it
was clear that something was up.

The 1919 World Series was corrupted by the players,
specifically Chick Gandil and Eddie Cicotte, who made the

initial approach to the gamblers, offering to throw the series
for $100,000. Eight White Sox players eventually took part in
the fix, either as active participants or as passive bystanders
aware of what was happening. Acting for Arnold Rothstein, a
New York gambler known as the Big Bankroll, Sport Sullivan
of Boston, and Abe Attell, a former boxing champ, paid up-
front money to Cicotte to lose game one.

Throwing nothing but soft pitches, Cicotte lost the first
game 9 to 1. In game two Lefty Williams also allowed the Reds
to hit him at will. By this time Comiskey knew something was
wrong, and some sportswriters, such as Hugh Fullerton of the
*Chicago Herald and Examiner,* Jim Crusinberry of the *Chicago
Tribune,* and the former pitcher Christy Mathewson, who was
also covering the series, suspected crooked play.

Comiskey reported his suspicions to Ban Johnson after
the first game but was rebuffed by the league president for
whining in defeat. The White Sox eventually lost the series 5
games to 3. Some baseball publications such as the *Sporting
News* chalked up the defeat to superior Cincinnati pitching
and overconfidence on the White Sox's part. Just after the
World Series the *Sporting News* rejected rumors of a fix in language that is especially telling about the ethnic sensibilities of
the era: "Because a lot of dirty, long-nosed, thick-lipped and
strong-smelling gamblers butted into the World Series" didn't
mean the games weren't cleanly played.

Fullerton reported that at least seven White Sox players
would not be back when the 1920 season started and hinted
that something was rotten about the Series. Comiskey tried to
allay these concern about gamblers and cover himself at the
same time by offering $10,000 to anyone who could provide
him with evidence that the Series had been fixed. But he did
not send out Series checks to the suspected players until
weeks after the season. Rumors that the World Series had

been corrupted continued into the off season, but nothing came of them.

## The Judge and the Bambino

THE 1920 SEASON was the greatest yet in baseball history. More than 9 million fans attended games that year, an increase of 2 million over the attendance record set 11 years earlier. Six teams established attendance records as baseball rebounded from the war. The New York Yankees went over 1 million, the first time that had happened in baseball history. Part of the reason for the Yankees' success was the impact of Babe Ruth, purchased from the Red Sox over the winter for $125,000 plus a loan from Colonel Ruppert of another $325,000 to Red Sox owner Harry Frazee. Frazee needed fresh funds to finance his latest Broadway musical, *No, No, Nanette.* At least this time Frazee had a winner, but he (and Boston) paid a terrible price for a show whose greatest attribute was the hit tune "Tea for Two."

Ruth hit an astounding fifty-four homers in 1920, a figure beyond anyone's imagination. More important, his homers dramatized baseball as nothing had ever done.

Records are usually broken incrementally. But Ruth's fifty-four home runs were an increase of 87 percent over his record-setting twenty-nine of the year before. Another way of looking at his feat is that he personally hit more home runs than any of the other fifteen major league teams. Fans flocked to see this new phenomenon, this freak of nature who played the game with such reckless abandon.

Ruth defies analysis. He was an original, an unbridled, bigger-than-life character whose approach to baseball changed the game forever. He swung the bat with gusto, putting his whole body behind it, an approach that reflected the uproarious quality of the decade he personified, the 1920s.

Among various explanations for the Ruth phenomenon are the banning of trick pitches in 1920, the greater use of new, cleaner balls, and a livelier baseball supposedly the result of using more tightly wound Australian wool. All of these may have played a part, but then why weren't there other Ruth-like figures hitting homers in 1920? The increase in home runs in the National League, which used the same ball as the American League, was negligible. The answer to Ruth's astounding record may be as simple as his powerful uppercut swing and his good fortune to be playing in a park, the Polo Grounds, with a short right-field porch easily reached by his towering fly balls. Of Ruth's fifty-four home runs, twenty-nine were hit in the Polo Grounds.

In a unique sense Babe Ruth changed baseball almost single-handedly and overnight. By swinging for home runs and uppercutting the ball, he went against the slashing, slap-the-ball style that had been favored since the formation of the two leagues. Comparing his statistics in 1920 with those of hitters in either league, this fact clearly emerges. The second-leading home run hitter in the American League in 1920 was George Sisler who hit 19. In the National League, Cy Williams of the Phillies led with 15, one more than "Irish" Meusel of the Giants. In slugging percentage Ruth set records that dwarfed all past figures. His .847 is still the highest in baseball history and was 225 points ahead of the next-leading figure in the American League and 288 better than the National League slugging leader, Rogers Hornsby.

Power hitters began to adopt the Ruth approach in the early 1920s, and home run records fell throughout the major leagues. Hornsby hit forty-two homers in 1922 while Ken

Williams of the Browns and Walker of the A's topped the thirty-five mark that same year.

In the decade Ruth hit fifty or more home runs four times, forty or more nine times. Six men—Lou Gehrig twice, Chuck Klein of the Phillies twice, Cy Williams, Mel Ott of the Giants, Hack Wilson of the Cubs, and Hornsby—topped the forty mark. Even Ty Cobb, the personification of the pre-Ruthian era, begrudgingly got into the power game. He hit three homers in a game in 1925 when he was thirty-eight years old and argued that if he had wanted to sacrifice his batting average he could have hit homers in bunches.

Cobb, who was jealous of Ruth's popularity, claimed that the Yankee slugger had ruined baseball by emphasizing home runs. Ruth's answer was simple and devastating—if he wanted to hit singles, he said, he would have batted around .600. An exaggeration, to be sure, but it is interesting to note that while swinging for the fences Ruth managed to achieve a lifetime batting average of .342, good enough for ninth place in baseball history.

While Ruth was shattering home run records, the Black Sox scandal became public in September 1920. On the 27th of the month a Philadelphia sportswriter, James Isaminger, interviewed Billy Maharg, one of the gamblers involved in fixing the series. Maharg gave information that implicated various members of the White Sox, and a Chicago grand jury was impaneled to investigate these charges as well as other rumors of attempts to fix games. In a matter of days, two of the Black Sox, Cicotte and Joe Jackson, confessed and implicated their teammates. The story was now out in the open.

The timing is interesting. The country was reeling from the Red Scare and a wave of bitter strikes when on September 16 a huge explosion took place on Wall Street that killed thirty-eight people, wounded two hundred, and did $2 million in damage. It seemed that nothing was sacred—not even baseball, now caught up in the worst scandal in its history.

It took almost six months for the Black Sox scandal to work its way through the courts and into the offices of the baseball establishment. The grand jury in Chicago indicted eight White Sox players, but they were acquitted in the trial that followed, partly because the ballplayers' confessions disappeared. After all, this was Chicago in the 1920s. Comiskey was a playing a desperate game. He wanted his players cleared, and he wanted any taint of scandal on his part dissipated. His approach worked until Judge Landis entered the picture.

In November 1920 the baseball owners, bitterly feuding among themselves, angry at Ban Johnson, and desperately worried that assorted gambling rumors would destroy their enterprise, adopted an idea first floated by Albert Lasker, a powerful backstage figure in Republican party circles in Chicago. Lasker suggested that professional baseball reorganize along modern business lines and that the ruling body of the game be headed by an outsider, someone with no links to one faction or another. He offered the names of such distinguished individuals as General John Pershing, former President Taft, Senator Hiram Johnson of California, Wilson's secretary of the treasury and son-in-law William Gibbs McAdoo, and Judge Kenesaw Mountain Landis. Their prominence implies how central baseball was to American life at the time. It is difficult to imagine a comparable collection being suggested as commissioner of baseball today. In November, as the Black Sox story was casting a pall over the game, the baseball owners, hat in hand, turned to Judge Landis.

Landis was offered the job on lucrative terms—a salary of $50,000 per year, a seven-year contract, and full powers to act as he saw fit in the interests of baseball. The organizational structure of the game was overhauled too, but in the final analysis all power rested with the new commissioner. The owners, always an obstreperous crew, agreed to a gag order of unparalleled import. They pledged themselves to "loyally support the commissioner in his important and difficult task, and we assure him that each of us will acquiesce in his decisions even when we believe them mistaken; and that we will not discredit the sport by criticism of him or one another." The *New York Times* summed up the attitude of most of the interested press by calling Landis's selection "fortunate" for baseball.

Kenesaw Mountain Landis (named for a Civil War battle in Georgia in which his father was wounded) was a small-town Midwesterner, a representative figure of the upwardly mobile Protestant lower middle class that transformed American society in the last half of the nineteenth century. Poorly educated, Landis managed to secure a law degree and briefly practice law with moderate success. His career took off after he managed the political campaign of a prominent Illinois Republican politician, Frank Lowden. In return, Lowden prevailed upon Theodore Roosevelt to name Landis to the federal bench for the Northern District of Illinois, which included the baseball center of Chicago. Landis found a home as a judge.

Theatrical, overbearing, dramatic, and unpredictable, Landis made a name for himself in the years before World War I. He forced John D. Rockefeller to testify in a celebrated anti-trust case and fined Standard Oil $29 million for violating the Sherman Anti-Trust Act. The case secured Landis's reputation as a Progressive jurist, though the decision was reversed by a higher court. During the Federal League wars, when the Baltimore baseball club sued the major leagues, Landis withheld a decision on the case until it was settled out

of court. Baseball officials remembered Landis's attitude, especially a statement he made from the bench at the time of
the Federal League case: "Any blows at the thing called baseball would be regarded by this court as a blow at a national institution."

Once in charge of baseball, Landis wasted no time in living up to his reputation as an activist. Shortly after the Black
Sox players were found innocent, Landis handed down a pro-
nouncement that would shape the governance of the game for
the next sixty years. "Regardless of the verdict of juries," he
intoned in his most dramatic manner, "no player that throws
a game; no player that sits in a conference with a bunch of
crooked players and gamblers where the ways and means of
throwing games are discussed, and does not promptly tell his
club about it will ever play professional ball."

Landis made no distinction between the clearly guilty,
such as Gandil and Cicotte, and those like Buck Weaver who
were aware of the fix but took no action. Some have criticized
Landis for the harshness of action, and there has been considerable sympathy for dupes such as the uneducated Jackson or
those who just went along. (Today there is even a movement
led by none other than Ted Williams to get Jackson elected to
the Hall of Fame—his lifetime batting average was .356.)

Landis's instincts in this case were correct. Baseball
could ill afford further gambling scandals. It had too many recent black marks and needed to reassure the people that it
was an honest game. Landis's harsh rulings and his success at
playing the tough but fair judge succeeded in doing precisely
that. The American public, led by the sportswriting fraternity, created the myth of the "people's commissioner," the
man who looked after the true interests of baseball. The writers also portrayed him as the ballplayers' commissioner, a
reputation that Landis was proud to have. "The club owners,"

he observed, "have the league presidents to look out for their interests." He would take care of the players' interests.

Between 1921 and 1927 Landis blacklisted twenty players for associating with gamblers or other questionable activities. No longer could a player skirt the line between honest play and cheating, as Hal Chase had done for years while playing for four different teams. Landis was the all-powerful dispenser of justice, answerable to no one.

The owners soon discovered they had created a monster in Landis, but they were powerless to control him because of his hold on fan loyalty. By their own greed and squabbling the owners had shown the need for an outside force to rule baseball. They had clearly demonstrated that they were no longer capable of doing so.

## Rube Foster and the Negro National League

WITH THE Black Sox scandal resolved, major league baseball experienced the greatest period of financial and popular success in its history. If any era of baseball deserves the designation "golden," it would be the years between 1921 and 1930.

Attendance rose to undreamed-of levels throughout baseball, both at the major and minor league levels. For the majors the decade average was 9.3 million per year, with the New York Yankees averaging more than a million a year. The Yankees reached the million mark seven times during the decade while Detroit did it once and the Cubs four times. Like Jack Dempsey's million-dollar gates in his championship fights, breaking the million mark had special significance in this decade where every rule and tradition was challenged.

Even the black community sought to duplicate the success of the major leagues. Blacks had played baseball at various levels, including collegiate and professional, throughout the game's early history. They were effectively banned from the professional game in the late 1880s as the nation resegregated after the Civil War. But they didn't stop playing baseball. Instead, during the next thirty years they organized their own leagues, formed teams of black players, and barnstormed throughout the country, often playing against white teams. Few of these enterprises lasted. In many ways the experience of black baseball mirrored what happened to white baseball in its early years. The various Negro leagues never adopted a reserve clause, and as a result players jumped from team to team with impunity.

The quality of play was often high, and many of the best black players could have made a major league roster. Frank Grant, who had a distinguished career in the 1880s with Buffalo of the International League and who later played with the Cuban Giants, was regarded by white players as an outstanding baseball talent. Another great player was John Henry Lloyd, a shortstop often called the "black Honus Wagner."

Early in the twentieth century John McGraw, while managing the Baltimore Orioles, recruited an outstanding hitter named Charlie Grant. McGraw tried to pass Grant off as an Indian, Tokohoma, but sportswriters blew his cover.

Blacks and their leagues struggled for survival in the early years of the century. Despite limited opportunities, a cadre of good players emerged so that it was only natural that someone would conceive of organizing a separate, if not quite equal, major league for black players.

In 1920 Rube Foster, a player-manager of the Chicago American Giants, helped establish the first black-administered sports league. Modeled in structure after the majors, Foster's Negro National League was made up of eight teams in six cities, Chicago, St. Louis. Kansas City, Detroit, Indianapolis, and Dayton. This Midwestern focus left out the cities with the two largest black communities in the United States in 1920, New York and Philadelphia. Two East Coast teams, the Atlantic City Bacharach Giants and the Hilldale club of Philadelphia, were affiliated with the Negro National League in a loose way so that Foster could tap the potentially lucrative Eastern market. All but one of the owners of these teams were black.

J. L. Wilkinson, the man who controlled the most successful of the barnstorming teams, the Kansas City Monarchs, was the only white allowed in the league.

In many ways Foster was imitating what Ban Johnson had done twenty-five years earlier—trying to create a successful baseball enterprise that would then be able to gain recognition from the major leagues. But he had a more difficult barrier to overcome: racial segregation.

It appears that Foster's league was financially successful in the 1920s and about as well run as earlier baseball leagues had been. One author estimates that in 1923, when the Negro National League was operating smoothly, each team in the league made a profit of around $5,000 while Foster received around $10,000 for his work. These figures, while small by major league terms in the 1920s, are comparable to professional baseball in the 1870s and 1880s.

Foster required all teams entering his league to secure a playing field so that a degree of league stability could be maintained. The playing rules followed those of major league baseball, though the Negro National League continued some practices being abandoned by the majors. More "inside" baseball was played—more hitting-and-running and much more base-stealing. Pitchers continued to use outlawed pitches, such as the spitball and the emery ball. The Negro League combined the power hitting of the Ruth era with the slap-and-dash style of the Dead Ball era.

The problems that plagued Foster's league were similar to those of professional baseball in its early years. Players jumped teams, franchises collapsed, schedules were not always met. The league remained unbalanced with no teams in the East where the black population was large and growing fast. A rival league, the Eastern Colored League, was formed in 1923 but was poorly run and collapsed in 1928.

In the early 1930s the onslaught of the depression and Foster's physical and mental deterioration followed by his death destroyed the Negro National League. But Foster had planted seeds that others would later harvest in the 1930s and 1940s, Black Baseball's "golden" age.

## The Long-ball Era

THE 1920S introduced a brand of baseball, centering on the home run, that persisted until the 1960s, when the stolen base returned to prominence. Every team in baseball, seeking to imitate the Yankees, moved away from playing for one run and depending on pitching to hold the lead.

Explanations abound for the rise in hitting that began around 1920. Along with Ruth's emphasis on the home run, pitchers lost an edge they had held for years. Reacting in part to the death of Ray Chapman in 1920 when he was beaned by a dirty, scuffed ball, major league baseball banned trick pitches. A handful of spitball pitchers were allowed to continue the practice for the rest of their careers, but all other trick pitches were outlawed. No longer could the pitcher "doctor" the ball at will by cutting it or rubbing it with emery or slippery elm to make the ball sail or dip. Umpires also were ordered to introduce new cleaner balls more often during the game so as to avoid the dark, tobacco-stained balls that characterized the Dead Ball era. There is also some evidence, not conclusive, that a livelier ball was introduced around 1920.

As a result, offense increased enormously during the decade. Batting averages rose from the .260s in 1919 to over .290 by the end of the decade. The .400 level was reached by individuals seven times in this period, compared to four times between 1901 and 1920.

As the home run suddenly became commonplace, pitching dominance faded. In the first twenty years of the century pitchers had recorded 30 victories seventeen times. No one did it in the 1920s. The ERA in baseball rose from 2.95 in the 1900–1920 era to 4.15 over the next dozen years.

Even old-fashioned managers such as John McGraw and Connie Mack, who had made their reputations by emphasizing pitching and defense, were forced to change with the times. Mack rebuilt his second great A's dynasty around a powerful offense. McGraw's last great team, the 1921–1924 Giants, featured some fine hitters—George "High Pockets" Kelly, "Irish" Meusel, and Frankie Frisch—but none of his pitchers could match Mathewson or "Iron Man" McGinnity.

The American League, which had dominated World Series play in the teens, continued to do so in the 1920s but by a narrower margin. The junior circuit had won eight of ten World Series in the teens but only six of ten in the 1920s.

In the first half of the decade McGraw's Giants defeated the Babe Ruth–led Yankees in 1921 and 1922, but in 1923 the American League began to assert itself, winning six of the next eight World Series.

This American League ascendancy arose from a Yankee dynasty built with Colonel Ruppert's money, the organiza-

tional genius of Ed Barrow, and the managerial skills of Miller
Huggins. The latter two recognized the offensive shift in baseball and built the Yankees accordingly.

Ruppert, Barrow, and Huggins constructed a perfect
team for the new brand of power baseball. Building around
Ruth, through trades and shrewd purchases they assembled
one of the greatest teams in baseball history. The Yankee outfield of the mid-1920s—Ruth, Bob Meusel, and Earle
Combs—may have been the greatest in baseball history.
Combs, for example, leading off between 1925 and 1930, averaged .333 with 122 runs scored. Meusel, a powerful right-
handed hitter, led the American League in homers once and
drove in 100 or more runs five times while compiling a career
average of .309.

In 1925 Lou Gehrig, signed off the campus of Columbia
University, became a regular first baseman for the Yanks and
immediately established himself as a power hitter second only
to Ruth. Between 1926 and 1930 he averaged .348 while
driving in 100 runs each season. In 1927, when Ruth hit his
record-breaking 60 homers, Gehrig hit 47, the second-highest
total in baseball by anyone other than Babe Ruth. The third-
leading home run leader, their teammate Tony Lazzeri, had
18. The Yankees hit 158 homers as a team, 102 more than the
second-place Philadelphia A's.

During the 1920s the Yankees won six pennants and three
World Series. Their success was a reflection of the last of the
ballparks built in the classic era of baseball construction,
1909–1923. Yankee Stadium was built on a ten-acre site for
which Colonel Ruppert paid the colossal price of $600,000.
Constructed across the Harlem River from the Polo Grounds
(from which the Yankees had been expelled by a jealous Mc-
Graw), Yankee Stadium was the greatest sports facility of its

day. Costing a little over $2 million, it was modern in a way that reflected the American ethos of the 1920s—massive, dwarfing all other ballparks. With a seating capacity of 65,000, it held 20,000 more than the next-largest park. On its opening in 1923 the crowd was estimated by the New York police at 74,200, an exaggeration but still 20,000 more than any baseball game had ever attracted.

No one in the National League could compete with the wealth of the Yankees. After 1924 the Giants drifted into hard times as McGraw aged badly. The team did not win another pennant for almost a decade. Success in the senior circuit was better distributed than in the American League. From 1925 on, three teams—the Pirates twice, the Cubs once, and the Cardinals three times—captured pennants. None could match the Yankees in overall talent, but the Cardinals developed a method to compensate for a lack of funds—the farm system.

The farm system was the brainchild of Branch Rickey, one of the few genuine innovators in baseball history. Nicknamed the Professor, Rickey was a mediocre catcher with a lifetime batting average of .239 who became associated with the Cardinals in 1917 as a manager and developer of talent. He recognized that he lacked funds to buy players, so he began constructing alliances with minor league teams who would develop players and keep a supply of talent flowing to the Cardinals.

The farm system concept reached fruition by the early 1930s and proved an economical as well as practical way to produce major league players. The Cardinal team that Rickey took over was terrible, finishing in the cellar in 1919 and seventh place the next year. Its talent was thin except for an angular shortstop/third baseman whom Rickey moved to second base. His name was Rogers Hornsby, and he was the pivot around whom Rickey constructed the closest thing to a Yankee-type dynasty in the National League in the mid-1920s.

In 1926 the Cardinals won their first pennant, led by Hornsby who between 1921 and 1925 had not only won five straight batting titles but had also averaged better than .400. The 1926 Cardinals included four future Hall of Famers: Hornsby, Jesse Haines, Chick Hafey, and Grover Cleveland Alexander. The Cardinals were good enough to beat a highly touted Yankee team in the World Series famous for Alexander's strikeout of second baseman Tony Lazzeri in the seventh game with the Series at stake.

Hornsby was eccentric and hard to handle. A sour, friendless individual who had no interests outside baseball save for betting on the races, Hornsby soon clashed with Rickey and the Cardinals' owners. He was shipped to the Giants in 1927 for Frankie Frisch but irritated McGraw and despite hitting .361 was traded to the Boston Braves. After winning another batting title in 1928 he was traded again, this time to the Cubs. In 1929 he helped them win a pennant, but he never again found a home in baseball. A brilliant baseball mind, his irascible personality and inability to get along with fellow players or owners doomed him to drift from team to team.

The last great club of the 1920s was Connie Mack's team of 1929–1931. In some ways it was a match for the great Ruth-led Yankees. Mack had broken up his last great team during the Federal League wars. He had expected to be able to rebuild quickly but instead fielded one of the worst teams in American League history from 1915 to 1921, finishing last for seven consecutive years. The 1915 A's not only finished last; their drop-off from the previous season, 56 games, was the greatest in baseball history. Mack's 1916 team had a winning percentage of .235, finishing 54½ games out of first place.

Mack slowly began to mold a new powerhouse. By 1922 he had escaped the cellar and had two pieces in place, Jimmy Dykes at third and Bing Miller in the outfield. He added Al Simmons in 1924, and pitcher Lefty Groves and catcher Mickey Cochrane in 1925 when the A's finished in second place. From 1926 on the A's were one of the top teams in the American League. Not yet a match for the Yankees, they closed the gap rapidly, winning 91 games in 1927 and 98 in 1928 when a young future Hall of Famer, Jimmie Foxx, became a regular. In late August they actually led the Yankees but then collapsed, though they still finished only 2½ games out of first.

In 1929 the A's began a string of three consecutive pennants, winning 313 games over that span, eleven more games than the Yankees had won between 1926 and 1928. An argument can be made that the A's were the better of the two teams. For one thing, there wasn't much difference in offense between the two teams; the Yankees had only a slight edge. But the Yankees could not match the A's pitching. They had no one quite as good as Grove, who was 79-15 in those years, leading the American League in strikeouts and ERA each season. Nor did the Yankees have a catcher the caliber of the A's team leader, the fiery Cochrane.

The A's success, however, reaffirmed one of Mack's theories about developing a successful team. He believed that the fans preferred an emerging, competitive club to one that was uniformly successful. As the A's won pennants between 1929 and 1931, their attendance declined each year by more than 200,000. By 1932 Mack was forced to sell off yet another great team in order to pay his bills.

Baseball's golden decade outlasted the beginning of the

depression by one year. 1930 was a great year for the major leagues as attendance passed the 10 million mark, a figure that would not be reached for another fifteen years. The net combined income of all major league clubs was $1,965,000 that year with a profit margin of 16.4 percent. 1930 is known as "the year of the hitter" in baseball history because so many hitting records were established, especially in the National League. Hack Wilson of the Cubs set the home run record for the senior circuit by hitting 56, a total that stood until 1998. He also drove in 190 runs, a figure that still stands. Ruth at 35 was on his way to breaking his home run record of 60 when he tore his hand on an outfield fence. He wound up with 49 for the year.

The two leagues established hitting records that have never been approached. The National League average was .303, the American .288. The most incredible statistic for the year might have been six National League teams hitting better than .300, led by the Giants at .319 and the Phillies at .315. The Giants finished third, the Phillies dead last while losing 102 games.

The surge in attendance again demonstrated that fans love to see high-scoring games. But baseball could not for long avoid the national economic decline that in the summer of 1930 began to deepen. Unemployment, which had averaged 3.7 percent in the 1920s, surged to 8.7 percent in 1930, foreshadowing the worst economic crisis in American history. Baseball was about to enter one of the darkest phases in its history.

*Branch Rickey, one of the game's great innovators.*

# Chapter 6

# BASEBALL IN DEPRESSION AND WAR, 1931–1945

THE GREAT DEPRESSION created the gravest economic crisis in the nation's history, intensified by the fact no one—no political party, no institution—seemed able to explain to the people why it had occurred. How to restore the nation's prosperity, how to revive the economy seemed beyond anyone's power. Confusion and anger led to scapegoating as the public sought easy answers and obvious villains. President Herbert Hoover, the banking system, European debtors, and Wall Street were among those blamed for the depression.

The American public, long noted for its optimism and confidence in the future, by late 1932 and early 1933 seemed to be foundering, without a sense of hope. The unemployment rate, always one of the key measures of the nation's economic health, reached 25 percent in 1933, highest in American history. The jobless figure never dropped below double digits until 1941 when rearmament began to sop up the pool of the unemployed.

Another measure of the economic vitality, Standard and Poor's index of stock prices, dropped from an average of 250 in October 1929 to less than 50 in early 1933, in the process wiping out all the gains the market had made since 1910. The American economy seemed to be in free fall, with recovery all but impossible. A kind of grim pessimism mixed with resentment and apathy settled over the nation.

The fifteen years from the onset of the depression until the end of World War II constitute one of major league baseball's most trying times. The problems that baseball confronted in these years called into question all the gains the sport had made since the turn of the century. Baseball's difficulties during this decade and half were intensified by the fast-fading memories of the great prosperity the game had experienced in the 1920s. The men who ran baseball in the years from 1931 to 1945 were essentially the same ones who had survived the Federal League wars, World War I, and the Black Sox scandal. They had basked in the good times of the 1920s without fully understanding what was happening. Now they were remarkably ill equipped to deal with the economic whirlwind that swept through the country, shattering their attendance.

At first owners cut salaries and other expenses, just as American business did, but these measures had little impact. Baseball's average salary of $7,500 in 1930 dipped to $4,500 six years later. Lou Gehrig, after more than a decade with the Yankees as a premier slugger, earned $36,000 in 1936, a figure less than half of Babe Ruth's peak salary of $80,000. In 1934 Ruth signed for $35,000.

Organized baseball was challenged as it never had been

before. It responded creatively, showing that the sport was still vital and alive. Commissioner Landis acted as a cheerleader for the game, noting that the problems of the nation were not baseball's fault. "The American people," he said in the midst of the depression, "love baseball. They will return as paying customers as soon as they have the money."

Attendance plummeted from the high of more than 10 million in 1930 to 5,964,000 four years later, a 41 percent drop. Never before had baseball experienced such a decline. The situation raised serious questions whether the game could survive under its 1903 organization. By 1934, with the depression in its fifth year and showing few signs of easing, a handful of teams were on the brink of collapse. The hapless St. Louis Browns, who had won nothing since the American League was organized, the Cincinnati Reds, the Phillies, and even Comiskey's vaunted White Sox had fallen on hard times. Overall major league teams lost $1.2 million in 1932 and $450,000 the next year.

The Browns attracted just 80,000 fans in 1933, slightly more than 100,000 the next season, and then under 100,000 for the next two years. The Phillies were in an equally bad state. Playing in the smallest, oldest, and most decrepit ballpark in the majors, Baker Bowl, which barely held 20,000, the Phillies were chronically short of cash and unable to compete with other teams in the majors. They had been the unwanted stepchildren of Philadelphia ever since they broke up the 1915 team that won the National League pennant. The last time the Phillies had outdrawn the A's at the gate was 1920; the next time was 1946.

The Phillies owner, William Baker, was often broke and unable to modernize his ballpark or pay for good players. When the Phillies did strike gold in player development, they almost immediately had to sell the player in order to pay bills.

Shortly before he died in 1930, Baker sent outfielder Lefty O'Doul, who had hit .398 and .383 in the previous two seasons, to the Dodgers for three nondescript players and $25,000 in cash. After Baker the team passed into the equally impecunious hands of Gerry Nugent. Nugent ran the Phillies on the same principles as Baker: develop the talent and then sell it before it commanded too high a salary.

Connie Mack's more successful A's were forced to adopt the same expedient during the depression. After winning three straight pennants, the A's fell on hard times beginning in 1932. Over the next three years Mack unloaded the stars who had led his 1929–1931 dynasty. He justified his action on the grounds of financial exigency and tried to lessen the impact on his club's chances by selling his players to teams that were lower in the standings than the A's. Al Simmons went to the White Sox, Cochrane to the Tigers, Grove and Foxx to the Red Sox—Hall of Famers all. Mack recouped enough for these players to pay off his debts and keep the team afloat. But the A's slipped to second in 1932, third in 1933, fifth in 1935, and finally into the cellar in 1936. Over the next decade the A's finished in the cellar no less than eight times.

The Phillies, under the financially strapped Nugent, finished in the basement eight times during this same period, giving Philadelphia the two worst teams in the major leagues for many years. In 1941 the Phillies record of 42–109, a .278 percentage, left them 62½ games out of first place. Even moving from Baker Bowl to Shibe Park in 1938 didn't help the Phillies, who continued to struggle on the field and at the gate. Not until Robert Carpenter, Jr., a scion of the DuPont family, bought the team in 1943 was there reason for optimism in Philadelphia.

During the 1930s the old guard who had run major league baseball for so many years began to pass from the scene.

Colonel Ruppert, Barney Dreyfuss of the Pirates, and Charles Comiskey died. Comiskey left the White Sox in his family's hands, but they were short of cash. The Red Sox received an infusion of new money in 1933 when Tom Yawkey, a multi-millionaire lumberman, bought the club. With the help of former star second baseman Eddie Collins, Yawkey began to rebuild the Red Sox. Reversing the team's role as a supplier of talent, especially to the Yankees, Yawkey used his bankroll to purchase established players—Grove, Foxx, outfielder Roger "Doc" Cramer, and third baseman Pinky Higgins from the A's; Joe Cronin, a shortstop, from the destitute Washington Senators. Cronin had been the player-manager of the Senators and in 1933 had led them to a pennant. He married Clark Griffith's niece after the 1934 season, and as a honeymoon present Griffith sold him for $250,000 to the Red Sox where he would continue as manager. With the Red Sox, Collins told Cronin not to worry, he and Yawkey would get him the players he needed to build a contender.

At the same time Collins poured more of Yawkey's money into developing talent at the minor league level. By the late 1930s the Red Sox farm system had produced two future Hall of Famers in second baseman Bobby Doerr and a young, skinny left-handed hitter with the sweetest swing since Shoeless Joe Jackson. He was Ted Williams.

The Red Sox started the steep climb to respectability by finishing with a .500 record in 1934, the first time since 1918 that the team had reached that level. In 1938 and 1939 they finished a distant second, constituting the closest thing the Yankees had to a rival in those years.

The St. Louis Browns remained hopeless throughout these years, starved of funds and lacking the organizational genius that Branch Rickey provided their rivals, the Cardinals. Rickey had once run the Browns, but he fell out with the team owner, the eccentric icehouse merchant Phil Ball, and moved to the Cardinals in 1917.

The Browns produced a decent club in the early 1920s, built around the immense talents of first baseman George Sisler, who hit .407 in 1920 and .420 in 1922. In 1922 they finished one game behind the pennant-winning Yankees and attracted 712,000 fans. Thereafter the team went into a decline from which it would not recover for a quarter-century, until 1944 when it won its one and only pennant. In 1930 attendance topped the 200,000 mark; it didn't reach this figure again for ten years.

Ball had taken over the Browns in 1916 and gave the team competent if eccentric leadership. He was one of the few owners skeptical of Judge Landis from the start. But he was short of funds, and his team couldn't compete with most clubs in the American League or with the crosstown Cardinals for fans. Ball died in 1933, and his successors had no more luck in competing with the wealthier clubs in the league. The Browns produced some fine players in the 1930s, such as the underrated third baseman Harlond Clift and first baseman George McQuinn. But throughout the 1930s the Browns were American League orphans.

Cincinnati had only begun to revive when the radio manufacturer Powel Crosley bought the team in 1933. Crosley breathed new life into the club and made a key recruitment when he hired Larry MacPhail to run the Reds. MacPhail was one of baseball's true innovators, an exotic character, part genius and part eccentric. His main claim to fame before baseball was an attempt to kidnap the kaiser during World War I. He missed the kaiser but took one of his ashtrays for his trouble.

After working as a college football referee, MacPhail turned his attention to baseball where made his reputation running the Louisville Colonels in the Cardinals chain. Always trying for something unusual, MacPhail sold season tickets to women for $3 to lure new fans, spruced up the ballpark, and introduced night baseball to the American Association. In 1930 his team actually outdrew the pennant-winning Cardinals by 30,000. He was responsible for convincing Crosley that the Reds were a worthwhile investment.

Among MacPhail's many innovations was the remodeling of the run-down Redland Field, now renamed Crosley Field. He poured money into player development, introduced night baseball to the majors, and hired a young Southerner, Red Barber, to broadcast the Reds games in hopes of creating a new audience for baseball.

By the late 1930s MacPhail had developed a pennant contender built around new young players such as first baseman Frank McCormick, a seven-time .300 hitter, outfielder Ival Goodman, and key additions through trades or purchases such as pitchers Bucky Walters, Paul Derringer, and catcher Ernie Lombardi. After three second-division finishes, in 1938 the Reds reached fourth place. Beginning the next season Cincinnati won two pennants and the 1940 World Series. By that time MacPhail was on his way to another rebuilding job, this time with the Brooklyn Dodgers.

Those teams that were taken over by new, wealthy owners such as Yawkey or Crosley survived the depression without difficulty. But overall, economic problems kept baseball on the edge of insolvency right up to World War II. Few teams showed a profit.

## Another Yankee Dynasty

FROM 1931 TO 1945 baseball was dominated by two great
teams, a Yankee dynasty in the American League and a superb Cardinals club in the senior circuit. Both were products
of high-class organizations built on different baseball principles. The Yankee dynasty of the 1920s ended in 1928 with the
death of their highly successful manager, Miller Huggins. For
three years, the Yankees still a powerful club, watched as Connie Mack's A's dominated the American League.

Huggins's successor was a former Yankee pitching ace,
Bob Shawkey. He had the unenviable job of controlling a team
on which the star player, Babe Ruth, believed he should be
manager. Ruth effectively undermined Shawkey, who quit
after the 1931 season. He was replaced not by the eager Ruth
but by Joe McCarthy, former manager of the 1929 pennant-
winning Cubs. Colonel Ruppert, the Yankee owner, didn't believe that Ruth had sufficient maturity or judgment to
manage a pennant contender.

McCarthy, a former minor league player, had managed in
the majors since 1926 with the Cubs. He was fired in 1931 by
the Cubs' owner, William Wrigley, who wanted Rogers
Hornsby as his new manager.

After McCarthy was hired by the Yankees, Colonel Ruppert told him, "I don't like second-place finishes." "Neither
do I," answered McCarthy, and immediately a bond was
forged between them.

In 1932 the Yankees won 107 games and easily beat the
A's for the pennant, but McCarthy had a difficult time managing because the team was divided into cliques with Ruth
providing the most trouble. He and McCarthy hardly spoke to
each other. McCarthy knew he couldn't restrain Ruth, who
was the biggest figure in baseball, but he hoped to outlast him.

When Ruth left the Yankees after the 1934 season, Mc-Carthy began constructing his kind of team of quiet professionals. Something of a martinet and a perfectionist, McCarthy built a team that was steady and deadly efficient. It took him three years and three second-place finishes before he had his kind of team in place.

With Ruth gone, Lou Gehrig, a player more in Mc-Carthy's mold, became the clubhouse leader. Bill Dickey, a talented catcher, virtually directed the team on the field. Frankie Crosetti at shortstop and Tony Lazzeri at second base formed a great double-play combination while Red Rolfe was a solid if unspectacular third baseman. The Yankee pitching staff was anchored by Lefty Gomez and Red Ruffing, two professionals who over the course of their careers won more than 450 games between them. Only the Yankee outfield was weak—until 1936.

That year a tall, quiet, almost painfully shy Italian American from California joined the Yankees. Joe DiMaggio was just twenty-one. Although he was plagued by a bad knee, the Yankees took a chance and signed him in 1933, paying the San Francisco Seals $25,000. Scouts raved about his talent and called him a "can't miss." He didn't.

DiMaggio was the last piece McCarthy needed to create a new Yankee dynasty. Beginning in 1936 the Yankees won four straight pennants and then went on to sweep all four World Series by a margin of 16 games to 3. After a two-year lapse they won three more pennants in a row and two more World Series for a record of five World Series won out of six played.

During these years the Yankees were without a serious rival. Their average margin of victory over the second-place team during those six years was 15½ games; the closest second-place team was 9 games behind. Few teams dominated the league as the McCarthy-led Yankees did.

George Weiss had been brought in by Ed Barrow to run the Yankee farm system. Weiss was a superefficient, coldly calculating character but a superb judge of baseball talent. Diffident almost to the point of inarticulateness, Weiss saw the value of developing talent. He had to fight the parsimonious Barrow, but Weiss was responsible for building the great Yankee farm system. The Newark Bears team he built in the late 1930s was one of the best in minor league history. Some baseball experts joked that Newark would finish third or fourth in the American League.

As Yankee veterans wore out, Weiss supplied a steady stream of a new blood. In 1937 Tommy Henrich, having been declared a free agent by Judge Landis, was added to the Yankee roster. The next year Charlie "King Kong" Keller took over the third outfield spot. The Yankees now had an outfield of Henrich, DiMaggio, and Keller that was a match for the great Yankee teams of the 1920s. In 1941, for example, these three combined for 94 homers, 332 runs batted in, and a batting average of .311.

When Tony Lazzeri began to slip at the plate and in the field, a young Joe Gordon was brought up in 1938. In his first five years in the majors he averaged 100 RBIs per season and in 1942 won the Most Valuable Player award. He was joined in 1941 by the young Phil Rizzuto to form a new double-play combination.

The 1936–1939, 1941–1943 Yankees were one of the great dynasties in baseball history. The team's tone was set by the quietly efficient Barrow, Weiss, and McCarthy. DiMaggio, Dickey, and Keller served as leaders on the field. When Lou Gehrig was forced to retire in 1939 after contracting amyotrophic lateral sclerosis, the Yankees adjusted without great difficulty. This was a feature of the Yankee teams. As one star wore out, another was ready to replace him. Gehrig replaced

Ruth, DiMaggio replaced Gehrig, and in 1951 a nineteen-year-old Mickey Mantle was ready to take DiMaggio's place as Yankee leader. That's how a dynasty works.

The St. Louis Cardinals were nurtured to success by Branch Rickey's brains and his unique creation, the farm system. Rickey developed teams that won two pennants in the 1920s, two in the 1930s, and four more in the 1940s. In six of these years the Cardinals also won the World Series.

In the 1930s Rickey honed his farm system to a fine edge. Drawing his talent largely from among poor farm boys and Southerners such as Pepper Martin, Dizzy and Paul Dean, Enos Slaughter, and Johnny Mize, Rickey stressed the importance of team depth. One of his favorite sayings was "Quality from quantity."

After winning three pennants as well as the World Series in 1931 and 1934, Rickey watched the Cardinals slip behind the Giants and Cincinnati Reds. In 1938 they dropped to sixth place, 17½ games behind the first-place Cubs. Rickey then initiated a classic rebuilding project. Older Cardinal players were traded away or sold off. New blood was brought in. Johnny Mize had joined the Cards in 1936; he took over first base and averaged close to .340 for the next four years. Enos Slaughter came up from the minors in 1938, catcher Walker Cooper and shortstop Marty Marion in 1940. The fine lefthander Howie Pollet joined the Cards in 1941 as did a slender left-handed hitting outfielder with a strange corkscrew stance—Stan Musial, who came up in late 1941 and became a regular the next year.

Beginning in 1939 the Cardinals were competitive again, finishing second to the Reds that year by 4½ games. They were a distant third in 1940 but came on strong in 1941, almost catching the red-hot Brooklyn Dodgers who won their first pennant in twenty years under the direction of their

McGraw-like manager, Leo Durocher. The Brooklyn regeneration was the handiwork of Larry MacPhail, who had taken over a bedraggled Dodger team in 1938 when he left the Reds. He spruced up Ebbets Field, purchased talented players from poorer clubs, and brought in Red Barber to broadcast the Dodger games. In 1940 MacPhail had built a powerful contender.

In 1942 the Cardinals, piloted by Billy Southworth, one of the most underrated managers of his era, won the first of three consecutive pennants. That year they beat a highly regarded Yankee team by taking four straight games after losing the first game of the World Series.

The Southworth-led Cardinals of the early to mid-1940s were one of the best teams in the National League in twenty-five years. They boasted great defensive players such as shortstop Marion and center fielder Terry Moore, superb hitters like Musial and Slaughter, and a solid, if unspectacular pitching staff anchored by rookie wonder Johnny Beazley as well as steady winners Howie Pollet, Mort Cooper, and Max Lanier. Between 1942 and 1944 the Cardinals won 316 games. Their average margin of victory over second-place teams was 11½ games.

After a falling out with the Cardinals' owner, a St. Louis car dealer named Sam Breadon, Rickey in 1942 left the club. He brought his talents to the Dodgers and replaced MacPhail, who had joined the army. With the Dodgers, Rickey's expertise in baseball matters, his unorthodoxy, and his willingness to challenge sixty years of baseball racism and sign a black player helped make the Dodgers the dominant team in the National League for the next quarter-century.

## Baseball Transforms Itself

IN *As You Like It* Shakespeare noted that "sweet are the uses of adversity." Professional baseball painfully discovered that truth during the years 1931–1945. In a curious way, the nation's problems led baseball to make changes that it otherwise would have postponed for years. Hard times energized the men who led baseball to open up the sport as never before.

Despite declining attendance, diminished profits, and the disruption caused by World War II, organized baseball transformed the game in these years. It was as if baseball needed the prod of adversity to discover new dimensions to the game.

Between 1931 and 1939 baseball adopted a unified Most Valuable Player award, introduced a highly successful All-Star Game, created the first sports Hall of Fame, spread the radio broadcasting of the game, and inaugurated night baseball.

These changes, among the most revolutionary in the game's history, were carried out by a usually conservative institution which was often profoundly suspicious of innovation. Yet each change was an important symbol by which baseball defined itself to the sports public. The changes helped save the National Game.

Baseball had flirted with a unified Most Valuable Player (MVP) award in 1911–1914, when the Chalmers Motor Car Company awarded a new car to the batting champion of each league. But the idea never found favor with the baseball establishment because control of the award was out of its hands. Also the value of the award opened up the possibility of cheating, as had happened in 1910 when certain St. Louis Browns players allowed Nap Lajoie to get hits in order to deprive the hated Ty Cobb of another batting title.

The two major leagues began issuing their own awards rather haphazardly in 1922, but not until 1931 did they systematize the process of recognizing outstanding achievement. Thus baseball stumbled onto one of the great public relations concepts in sports—awards for single-season greatness, which thus draw attention to the game. Perhaps the success of Hollywood's new Academy Awards in 1927–1928 encouraged baseball to create a similar process of recognition.

The new MVP award in 1931 was the work of the Baseball Writers' Association of America, the organization created early in the twentieth century by the men who covered professional baseball. From 1931 to 1945 the writers vied with the prestigious *Sporting News* in choosing the best player in each league. Their choices were often the same. Between 1932 and 1939, for example, the two organizations agreed on the MVP award in both leagues every year but one. In 1945 the two awards were finally unified, with the baseball writers taking over the voting.

The concept was a brilliant success, attracting attention to the game after the season ended. More important, it promoted arguments about the game and its players, the essence of the so-called Hot Stove League. Over the years the concept was expanded to include a Rookie of the Year, a Manager of the Year, Cy Young awards for the outstanding pitchers, Golden Glove awards for the best defensive players, and so on. All of these concepts were built onto the MVP award idea and helped spread the popularity of baseball. Other sports soon adopted the idea.

In 1933 an equally creative concept was virtually forced on baseball. Arch Ward, a sportswriter for the *Chicago Tribune,* the most influential newspaper in the Midwest, suggested that a game be played in mid-season with teams made up of the best players in the two major leagues. Ward's idea wasn't new; such games had been organized before on special occasions to raise money. Chicago was holding its Century of Progress Exhibition, and Ward thought that having a game of All-Stars would help dramatize the event.

With the backing of his powerful paper, he took the idea to Will Harridge, the unobtrusive president of the American League whose office was in Chicago. Making a powerful case, Ward argued that an All-Star Game would showcase baseball's best players and demonstrate that the sport was still vibrant. Ward suggested that profits from the game could go to the Players Charity Fund, an organization created to help needy players. Finally, Ward said, the game should stimulate fan interest in baseball at a time when attendance was in a steep decline. He suggested allowing the fans to vote for the players to appear in the game. As it turned out, more than half a million ballots were cast for the first All-Star Game held in Chicago at Comiskey Park.

The normally conservative Harridge liked the idea and sold it to Commissioner Landis, who at first was suspicious of a concept that originated not with baseball officials but with a sportswriter.

To manage the two All-Star squads, baseball drew on its historic past. Connie Mack, the longest-serving manager in baseball history, led the American League team while John McGraw came out of retirement to guide the National Leaguers. This move brilliantly linked the 1933 game with two men who had helped define the sport in the 1890s. Baseball was discovering how important it was to highlight its place in America's past.

The game itself was a huge success. Forty-nine thousand fans attended; gross receipts were just under $57,000, of which $46,500 went to the Players Charity Fund. The American League won and, appropriately enough, Babe Ruth, 38 years old, overweight, and fading fast, hit the first home run in All-Star Game history

The All-Star Game was quickly adopted as an annual institution by major league baseball. Again, the success of the idea can be seen in the way it has been copied by every other sport. But baseball's All-Star Game is the only one that is truly competitive because it is built into the historic rivalry of the two major leagues.

Baseball's most original idea in the 1930s was the establishment of a Hall of Fame. The concept had been talked about for years, but nothing came of it. In the 1920s the owners had given serious thought to establishing a Hall of Fame in Washington, D.C., but Congress refused to vote funds.

The idea lay dormant until a confluence of events revived it in the midst of the depression. Alexander Cleland, an executive with the Clark Foundation, a charitable organization in Cooperstown, New York, remembered that according to a study commissioned by Albert Spalding, Cooperstown was the supposed site of the invention of baseball in 1839 by Abner Doubleday. Cleland knew nothing of the controversy over the role of Doubleday versus Cartwright as the creator of modern baseball. But Cleland did see the possibility of using Cooperstown's link to baseball as a way of attracting tourists to this resort far off the beaten track in upstate New York. What he had in mind was a museum of baseball history filled with artifacts from every era of baseball's past.

The Clark Foundation liked his idea and in 1935–1936 authorized Cleland to approach major league baseball through Ford Frick, president of the National League. As a former sportswriter and public relations man, Frick immediately grasped the possibilities of Cleland's idea, but he broadened the concept of a baseball museum to a Hall of Fame that would recognize the greats of the game.

Like the All-Star Game, this was a brilliant concept. Halls of Fame existed in the United States but usually with a distinct political dimension. A sports Hall of Fame was something unique. Judge Landis was not as enthusiastic about the project as Frick, but he discovered that baseball owners liked the idea. The Hall of Fame would call attention to baseball's past and by honoring the game's greatest players would stimulate fan interest at a time when baseball needed all the popular support it could get.

A great many problems were overcome with the financial aid of the Clark Foundation and the support of the baseball establishment to construct a Baseball Hall of Fame in Cooperstown. It opened in 1939, the so-called centenary of baseball's invention by Abner Doubleday.

The first group of honorees generated broad agreement. Those named by the Baseball Writers on their first three ballots in 1936, 1937, and 1939 were a representative sample of baseball's greatest players. Ty Cobb, Babe Ruth, Christy Mathewson, Walter Johnson, and Honus Wagner were the first players chosen, with little argument. But subsequent ballots leading up to the opening of the Hall of Fame did provoke discussion among fans and writers. What about the pre-1900 players—shouldn't they be represented? How about the nonplayers who contributed so much to the game—shouldn't they have a place? This kind of public exchange was precisely what baseball wanted.

At the opening ceremony of the Hall of Fame in May 1939, the first among baseball's greats were enshrined in the new sports Valhalla. Along with the initial group they included such stars as Napoleon Lajoie, George Sisler, Grover Cleveland Alexander, Tris Speaker, and two managers, Connie Mack and John McGraw. Nonplayers included Alexander Cartwright, Morgan Bulkeley, the first president of the Na-

tional League, and Henry Chadwick, the real father of baseball writing.

The ceremony, witnessed by a crowd of between 3,500
and 4,000, was a huge success. Baseball realized it had stumbled onto a great idea for both advancing the game and per-
petuating the myth of its uniqueness. Today the installation
of new honorees to the Hall attracts tens of thousands of fans
and great publicity for baseball. No other sport comes close to
promoting this interest in honoring its past stars.

The 1930s saw the beginning of the wide-scale broadcasting of baseball on radio as well as the first tentative attempts
to televise the game. Radio broadcasting had been around
since the 1920s, but few teams took advantage of the new
technology either to make a profit or to spread the popularity
of the game. Professional baseball approached radio broadcasting with what can only be called passivity.

Initially the baseball owners feared that radio broadcasts
would damage attendance, a view endorsed by the *Sporting
News*. The Bible of Baseball was consistently skeptical about
baseball broadcasting. For years it warned that baseball was a
game better seen than heard. Then it argued that fans would
stay home and listen to the games for free; teams would play
before empty stadiums. Judge Landis too needed convincing,
believing that radio would come to control baseball. In fact,
baseball broadcasts actually created new fans and spread the
popularity of the game far beyond major league cities. The St.
Louis Cardinals and Chicago Cubs were the first to recognize
this possibility and thus created large followings in their own
areas of the Midwest.

In the 1930s each major league team was free to make its
own plans for radio. Some allowed stations to broadcast without licensing fees; others banned all broadcasts, even re-
creations of games. This situation began to change in 1934

when Commissioner Landis negotiated a four-year, $400,000 agreement with the Ford Motor Company to sponsor the World Series. When that contract ran out in 1939, the Gillette Safety Razor Company took over as sponsor of the World Series broadcasts. In 1935 Landis added the All-Star Game for a fee. Once the baseball owners saw the potential financial rewards, they refused to let the commissioner dictate their local radio practices. They also insisted that announcers serve as promoters of baseball, not true reporters.

By 1936 only the three New York teams did not broadcast their games, believing this was necessary in order to sustain their attendance. Most teams negotiated deals providing for sponsored radio broadcasts, in 1939 averaging around $55,000 per team. The sponsors tended to be manufacturers of male-oriented products—gasoline, beer, tobacco, breakfast cereal. General Mills went into baseball broadcasting in a major way with Wheaties as its lead product. Fourteen of the sixteen major league teams had General Mills as a sponsor. An entire generation of boys grew up hoping that eating Wheaties would make them great hitters like Babe Ruth or Lou Gehrig, whose pictures appeared on the Wheaties box.

In 1939 Larry MacPhail, who had taken over the Dodgers, announced that he would no longer abide by the nonbroadcasting rule in New York. That season he sold the rights to the Dodgers' games for $77,000. Given the fact that the average salary in the majors was a little over $7,000 that year, radio paid for almost 40 percent of the Dodger payroll.

MacPhail had had considerable success in Cincinnati with radio and had introduced baseball's first great announcer, Walter "Red" Barber, to the sport. He brought Barber with him to Brooklyn, intending to use his talents to build a new fan base to challenge the supremacy of the Yankees and Giants in the New York area. These rivals were forced to rethink their policy, and by the end of the depression decade every team broadcast its games.

The last of the great innovations of the decade was night baseball. Night games had been tried in the past with some success, and in the early 1930s the Negro leagues had adopted the idea. Most technical difficulties had been ironed out long before this time. The minor leagues had also experimented with night baseball. When MacPhail worked in the Cardinals' minor league system he discovered that night games outdrew day games by a wide margin.

Despite its attendance problems in the early 1930s, major league baseball at first rejected night games out of hand. The *Sporting News* called the idea "the ruination of baseball" and a fantasy that would fade because of inherent technical problems. Baseball, it declared, should be played in the daylight.

In 1934, when MacPhail moved to Cincinnati, he convinced Powel Crosley to try night baseball. It took Crosley a year to gain approval from other National League owners, most of whom remained skeptical. At the December 1934 winter meetings, they approved a night baseball experiment by a vote of 5 to 3. But they regarded the concept as a novelty at best, one that would fade in a few years. On May 24, 1935, the Reds played the Phillies in the first night game in major league history. These two uncompetitive teams drew 20,400 fans in an otherwise meaningless game—an attendance almost seven times Cincinnati's average weekday figure.

MacPhail even convinced President Roosevelt to throw a switch in Washington that turned on the lights in Cincinnati. The Reds were allowed to schedule only six more night games that season, which drew 110,000 fans. The seven night games averaged 18,700 while the remaining home dates averaged 4,300. Within a couple of years the race was on to add lights in almost every major league park. By 1941 there were only two holdouts in the National League, the Chicago Cubs and the Boston Braves. The Cubs were preparing to add lights in 1942 when World War II stopped them—for more than forty years. In the American League only the Yankees, Tigers, and Red Sox, all successful teams with rich owners, rejected night baseball. They fell in line just after the war.

Contrary to many predictions, night baseball did not destroy the essence of the game. Statistically the difference between day and night games proved to be insignificant. And the concept was popular with fans who flocked to night games throughout the major leagues. During World War II President Roosevelt suggested playing games at night so that war workers could see baseball in their leisure time. Always eager to associate baseball with anything patriotic, the game's establishment gladly complied. By the end of the war night baseball was completely accepted by fans, sportswriters, and baseball authorities alike.

## Baseball's "Good War"

FOR MAJOR LEAGUE BASEBALL, World War II was a good war, unlike its experience in 1917–1918 when the game almost closed down. By 1941 baseball was truly America's game, one of the ways in which Americans defined themselves. In particular, for most white men, baseball provided a deep sense of continuity in the midst of vast social, political, and cultural change.

After Pearl Harbor the federal government was sympathetic to baseball's problems. On January 14, 1942, Judge Landis wrote to President Roosevelt pledging baseball's patriotic support of the war and asking the president if baseball should disband for the duration. Landis was worried that the game would seem frivolous amidst the national crisis and the intense patriotic purpose that swept the country after Pearl Harbor.

Roosevelt answered the next day and gave baseball a green light to continue play. "I honestly feel," the president wrote, "that it would be best for the country to keep baseball going. There will be fewer people unemployed and everybody will work longer hours and harder than ever before. And that means that they ought to have a chance for recreation and for taking their minds off their work more than before."

Baseball continued for the duration of the war with the exception that in 1945 no All-Star Game was played. Everything else remained the same. The season was not abbreviated as it had been during World War I—it remained at 154 games. The World Series was played every season.

But there were some obvious differences. Major league rosters were depleted by the military draft. More than a thousand former and current major leaguers served in the military during World War II, including most of the best players of the time. In 1941 Hank Greenberg and Bob Feller were the first of the stars to enter military service. 1942 was the last "normal" season, after which the major leagues lost most of their better players, including Joe DiMaggio and Ted Williams. By 1943 baseball was forced to dip into the ranks of older, even retired players and bring up youngsters who should have been playing in the minors. In the words of one author, baseball was now in the hands of the old, the halt, and even the lame. Hod Lisenbee, 45 years old and out of the majors since 1936, appeared in 31 games for Cincinnati in 1945. Sixteen-year-old Tommy Brown played in 46 games and had 146 at bats with the 1944 Dodgers. In 1945 one of the starting outfielders for the St. Louis Browns was the one-armed Pete Gray.

Latin players, because they were draft-exempt, found themselves in demand during the war. Clark Griffith of the Washington Senators liked having Latin players on his payroll because they came cheap. In 1944 he had four Cubans under contract while Connie Mack, his counterpart in keeping costs low, had two.

But overall the disappearance of talent affected the quality of baseball in both leagues for three years, 1943–1945, depressing it to a level not seen since the Dead Ball era. In 1943 run production dropped to under 4 per game, lowest since 1918. In 1943 only one National Leaguer, Bill Nicholson with 29, hit more than 20 home runs. The American League had just three. The next year Nick Etten of the Yankees led the American League with 22 homers, the lowest figure since 1918. In 1945 Snuffy Stirnweiss of the Yankees won the batting title with a .309 average, a figure not seen since 1905. Statistically the National League held up better than the American offensively, but both leagues suffered a major decline during the war years.

The junior circuit hit 734 homers in 1941, but that figure steadily declined every season through 1945. That season the American League totaled just 430 home runs, or 56 per team. The National League home run total held up better but did not reach the 1941 level in any war year.

Baseball attendance had just begun to recover from the depression in 1940–1941 when the war drove the figure down again. In 1943 fewer fans turned out than in any year since 1935. Then attendance began a slow rise in 1944 and a big jump in 1945 to a record-setting 10.8 million. It is difficult to explain the rise in 1944 and 1945. Neither season was a particularly exciting one, though the pennant race in the American League in 1944 was a close one with the Browns edging the Tigers by 1 game. The next year the Tigers won the pennant by a margin of just 1½ games. Only the Tigers drew well in these two seasons, exceeding the 1 million mark in 1945.

Perhaps the American public turned to baseball in the last years of the war as a distraction from battlefront news. Baseball meant normalcy, something the American public longed for during World War II.

*Jackie Robinson stealing home.*

# Chapter 7

# NO GOLDEN AGE: BASEBALL, 1946–1960

IF BASEBALL had a good war, it enjoyed the postwar period even more. Like the nation, baseball boomed after the war, experiencing for four years one of the sport's greatest sustained bursts of prosperity.

As the war drew to a close, the issue that haunted many Americans was a fear that the nation would see the depression return. The demobilization of twelve million military personnel and the disappearance of ten million war jobs intensified that concern. The prosperity of the war years had not banished the ghost of the depression. While the government shared these fears, it was also concerned about inflation as pent-up wartime savings (estimated at $136 billion) were released into the economy. During the war the government had managed to hold inflation to less than 2 percent per year.

Neither of these fears proved real, though inflation surged briefly in 1946 as wage and price controls were ended over President Truman's vigorous protests. From 1945 to 1949 the inflation rate was close to 4 percent, but it was offset by the enormous postwar prosperity that swept through the American economy. The United States was about to enter what *Fortune* magazine described as "the dream era . . . what everyone was waiting through the blackouts for . . . the Great American Boom."

Reconversion to peacetime production created fewer problems than anticipated. Companies began producing consumer products such as cars, refrigerators, washers, and dryers in record numbers while the greatest home-building program in American history was launched. The spread of Levittowns and their suburban cousins created a whole new home-owning society in the United States. The country's prosperity over the next two generations reached undreamed-of levels. By 1956 the United States, with just 6 percent of the world's population, produced two-thirds of the goods manufactured around the globe.

Professional baseball looked forward to the postwar era, recognizing that its fans wanted to see the stars of the game back on the field. Will Harridge, president of the American League, estimated that 260 former major leaguers would be available by the opening of the 1946 season, including such stars as Joe DiMaggio, Ted Williams, Stan Musial, and Johnny Mize. The owners had been pleasantly surprised by the attendance record established in 1945 and expected an even better year the next season. They were further encouraged by the continuation of the contract with Gillette to pay $150,000 to sponsor the World Series—50 percent more than had been paid in the past.

The first normal season since 1941 turned out to be an even better one for baseball than anyone had hoped. The major leagues drew 18.5 million fans in 1946, almost 7.7 million more than the previous season, and a new record. This

71 percent increase was the greatest one-year improvement in baseball history. Eleven of the sixteen teams set new attendance records, with some, like the woeful Phillies, drawing a million fans for the first time. With the return of their established stars DiMaggio, Joe Gordon, Phil Rizzuto, Charley Keller, and Tommy Henrich, the Yankees saw their attendance figure jump from 880,000 to more than 2.2 million, the first time any team had drawn over 2 million fans. This is remarkable considering that the Yankees had a terrible season in 1946, finishing in third place 17 games behind the pennant-winning Red Sox. DiMaggio failed to hit .300 for the first time in his career while the steady Joe Gordon failed to regain his prewar form, hitting just .210. After the season he was traded to Cleveland for pitcher Allie Reynolds, who went on to become one of the anchors of the Yankee dynasty of the late 1940s and early 1950s.

For three consecutive years the major leagues enjoyed record-breaking attendance figures, peaking in 1948 at 20.9 million. In those three years every team in the American League broke its previous attendance record while all but Cincinnati and Chicago did so in the senior circuit. The Cleveland Indians, in capturing their first pennant in twenty-eight years in 1948, drew 2.6 million fans, a figure not bettered for thirty-two years until the 1980 Yankees. In the National League the 1947 Brooklyn Dodgers, aided by the smashing success of Jackie Robinson ending baseball's color bar, drew 1.8 million fans, an average of 23,000 per home date in a ballpark that barely held 32,000.

The success of the major leagues in these years was aided by three dramatic pennant races in the National League. The 1946 season ended with the Dodgers and Cardinals in a tie, necessitating the first playoff in major league history. The Cardinals won it and went on to victory in the World Series over the highly favored Red Sox. In 1947 the Dodgers edged the Cardinals by 5 games while a third team, the formerly hapless Braves, won in 1948 by a margin of 6½ games.

Three different teams won pennants in the American League between 1946 and 1948, but two of those races were runaways. The Red Sox pulled away early in 1946 winning the pennant by 12 games. The next season the Yankees reeled off nineteen straight wins in June, effectively ending the pennant race. 1948 witnessed a great struggle in the junior circuit. As late as August four teams—the Yankees, Red Sox, Indians, and even the once lowly A's—were separated by just a few games. The Red Sox and Indians ended the season in a tie with the Indians handily winning a one-game playoff, the first in American League history.

But everything wasn't rosy for major league baseball after the war. The threat of a new league surfaced in 1946 when the Pasquel brothers, Mexican millionaires, raided the majors for players for their league south of the border. With astounding financial offers, the Pasquels revived long-forgotten memories of the destructive Federal League wars. Their plan was to lure thirty to forty players to Mexico every season and thus in a few years to establish the validity of their already thriving Mexican League. It had turned a profit of $400,000 in 1945, but the Pasquels recognized that with the return to baseball normalcy they would be competing with American major league stars.

The Pasquels began their raid during spring training in 1946, signing some marginal Latin players such as Nap Reyes of the Giants and Bobby Estalella of the A's. They snatched Danny Gardella away from the Giants and signed the Dodgers' Luis Olmo, who had hit .313 in 1945, from under Branch Rickey's nose with a contract for $40,000 for three years. Rumors of the money being offered spread rapidly through the spring training camps. Dodger catcher Mickey Owen received a signing bonus of $12,500 while the Cardinals' pitchers Max Lanier and Freddie Martin were also lured away.

The sums being talked about seemed unreal. Stan Musial, then earning $13,500, was offered a salary of approximately $75,000. To show they were serious, the Pasquels offered him five certified checks of $10,000 each. An even more remarkable offer was made to the best pitcher in baseball, the Tigers' Hal Newhouser. According to one source, Newhouser, then among the highest-paid players in the majors at $45,000, was offered a bonus of $300,000 and a three-year contract worth $200,000.

The owners feared disaster. The new commissioner, A. B. "Happy" Chandler, a former Kentucky governor and U.S. senator who had succeeded Judge Landis in 1944, took a page from the former czar's book: he threatened to blacklist any player who breached his contract and signed with the Mexican League by banning him from the major leagues for five years. But what killed the Pasquels' plan was not the actions of organized baseball but rather the stories that filtered back from the Mexican League about its strange foods, terrible playing conditions, language problems, poor living arrangements, and unruly fan behavior. In a few months some of the major leaguers who had jumped were clamoring to return to the majors, admitting they had made a mistake. Not everyone who had stood fast in the United States was forgiving. Marty Marion, the star shortstop of the Cardinals, said when he heard that Mickey Owen wanted to return to Brooklyn: "Owen jumped his team to go down there for that big money; now let him stay there."

By the end of 1947 the threat from the Mexican League had dissipated. Chandler refused to lift his ban on the "Mexican jumpers," as the players were called. Some talented play-

ers had their careers curtailed by his action, in particular Sal
Maglie, a Giant farmhand who showed great promise as a
pitcher. In 1949 major league baseball lifted the ban because
of a lawsuit filed by Danny Gardella. Chandler recognized
that Gardella might win, thus jeopardizing baseball's unique
legal status. Many of the jumpers returned, but only Maglie
went on to have a distinguished career. Baseball had dodged
the Mexican threat, but an even greater challenge arose in
1946 with the first serious attempt to unionize baseball players in thirty years.

Shortly before the 1946 season Robert Murphy, a former
examiner for the National Labor Relations Board, formally
registered his union, the American Baseball Guild, and then
toured the various spring training camps to enroll players.
The baseball owners took Murphy seriously because the union
movement in America was both thriving and militant since
the New Deal. During the war the nation's two largest
unions, the American Federation of Labor and the Congress of
Industrial Organizations, had increased their membership by
more than 60 percent. By 1946 union members made up
36 percent of the nonagricultural work force while union
membership reached an all-time high.

Murphy outlined a simple plan to benefit the players, featuring a minimum salary of $6,500, a percentage of the sale
price if they were sold, and the right to arbitration in certain
disputes. He steered clear of any discussion of the reserve
clause and tried to project a serious, moderate image.

Murphy frightened baseball's owners. By exaggerating
his success in enrolling players, he hoped to convince the owners to recognize his union. He claimed that by mid-season he
had substantial membership in ten or eleven major league
teams and a majority signed on four or five.

But Murphy was bluffing. On June 7 he forced a vote of

the Pittsburgh Pirates, hoping that players in this most unionized city in the majors would support the Guild as their bargaining agent. He lost the vote after the Pirate management worked aggressively to beat back his challenge. Frankie Frisch, the Pirate manager, threatened to suit up old Honus Wagner to play if the players went on strike. The Guild movement gradually disintegrated. By the end of the year Murphy was reduced to trying to organize professional hockey players, then a sport of lesser interest in the United States.

Murphy may have failed, but he caused the baseball owners to take players' complaints seriously for the first time in years. During July and August representatives from the players and owners met to forge a new working agreement. Called with typical exaggeration by New York sportswriter Dan Daniel "Baseball's Magna Carta," it did meet some of the players' demands. It established a minimum salary of $5,000, provided players with $500 for expenses if traded or sold to another club, and increased spring training money for the players, thereafter known as Murphy Money. Most important, the agreement established baseball's first pension program funded by money from the All-Star Game and radio broadcasting rights.

In effect, major league baseball had thwarted unionization for twenty years. With most of the players sharing the individualist outlook of the times and focusing on what they would do after their baseball career was over, the minimum salary and pension program satisfied their aspirations. In 1956 the Major League Baseball Players Association was created to protect these interests. A prominent New York attorney, Norman Lewis, served as the association's first director. He did so in a low-keyed manner, cooperating with the owners rather than adopting confrontational tactics.

## Integrating Blacks

WHILE professional baseball thrived in the years immediately after the war, the sport was confronted with problems
that nearly overwhelmed it. The generation from the end of
World War II until the early 1960s witnessed the most pro-
found transformation in baseball history: the challenge of integration, the threat from the new medium of television, and
the first major franchise shifts in fifty years.

The racial barrier that had kept blacks out of major
league baseball since the 1880s was at last lifted. The agent of
this dramatic change was Branch Rickey of the Dodgers, a curious blend of huckster, philanthropist, and baseball guru.

Rickey, nicknamed the "Mahatma" after Gandhi because
of his frequent moral lectures, had come to the Dodgers from
the Cardinals in 1942 when Larry MacPhail joined the army.
Rickey had turned the Cardinals into a baseball powerhouse,
chiefly by developing the minor league farm system, called
Rickey's "Chain Gang" by some writers. He began immediately to build on the groundwork laid by the innovative
MacPhail. During the war, instead of cutting back on expenses, Rickey signed as much raw baseball talent as he could
find. Although he would be denied their services for the duration of the conflict, he counted on having a pool of superior
talent available to the Dodgers once the war ended.

Rickey also recognized that there was one untapped well
of talent remaining in the country: black players who had
demonstrated in the Negro leagues that they could play baseball on a par with the best major leaguers. Rickey was determined to mine this "black gold" first, even if it meant defying
the baseball establishment in the process. He ordered the
scouting of the Negro leagues during the war, looking for the
right player to be the first black on the Dodgers.

There were more talented and better-known players in the Negro leagues, but Rickey's attention was drawn to Jackie Robinson of the Kansas City Monarchs. Robinson was a skilled player, but more important he had the qualities that Rickey was looking for in a trailblazer. He was mature, poised, college educated, and intensely focused on success. In October 1945 Rickey shocked the sporting world by announcing that Robinson had been signed to a Dodgers contract to play for their top minor league team, the Montreal Royals. In his usual tightfisted manner, Rickey signed Robinson for a bonus of $3,500 plus $600 a month for the 1946 season.

The decision was greeted with skepticism by the baseball establishment. After Robinson won the batting title at Montreal and was named league MVP in 1946, the *Sporting News* suggested that he was playing over his head and "that his crusading zeal to pave the way for others of his race . . . actually increased his ability." The paper doubted he could perform at the major league level. Bob Feller claimed with remarkable obtuseness that Robinson was too muscled to play in the major. If he were white, Feller said, "I doubt if they would consider him big league material." (A muscular upper body hadn't held back Jimmie Foxx or Lou Gehrig.)

Robinson proved himself in his first year, winning Rookie of the Year honors and helping lead the Dodgers to their first pennant since 1941. More significant, he opened the eyes of other baseball owners by proving to be the greatest gate attraction since Babe Ruth. The Dodgers set a new attendance record that season partly because of Robinson's appeal. Over the next few seasons Robinson proved he had All-Star ability. In 1949 he won a batting title and was named league MVP. He became one of the catalysts in the great Dodger dynasty of the 1950s. Red Schoendienst of the Cards once observed with some exaggeration that without Robinson the Dodgers would have been a second-division team—a nice compliment to Robinson but scarcely true of a team that included Pee Wee Reese, Gil Hodges, Duke Snider, Roy Campanella, and Don Newcombe.

Major league baseball typically was slow to cash in on black talent. The Dodgers led the way, helped by Robinson's prominence. By 1949 they had two other skilled black players on their roster, catcher Roy Campanella, a future Hall of Famer, and Don Newcombe, a powerful right-handed pitcher.

Bill Veeck, owner of the Cleveland Indians and a baseball innovator and showman of the first order, broke the color barrier in the American League in 1947 by signing Larry Doby. The next season he added the greatest draw of the Negro leagues, pitcher Satchel Paige. Veeck was jealous of the credit Rickey had earned for integrating baseball, an idea that the unpredictable Veeck had been toying with for some time. Doby and Paige contributed to the Indians winning the 1948 pennant and the World Series. Doby batted .301 that season while the ageless Paige won six of seven decisions with an ERA of 2.48 and two shutouts—not bad for a forty-two-year-old rookie.

The Giants, hoping to match the success of the Dodgers in attracting a new fan base in the New York area, joined the pursuit of black talent in 1949, signing Monte Irvin who was considered the best hitter in the Negro leagues. Irvin, though thirty years old, proved to be a fine right-handed hitter and outfielder, but the Giants really struck gold when they signed a teenage phenom named Willie Mays. Mays didn't make it to the majors until 1951, but he quickly established himself with Mickey Mantle as the best center fielder of his generation and the first black superstar. Mays helped the Giants win a pennant in 1951, though Irvin was the real star of that team. In 1954 Mays, then twenty-two, led the Giants to their first

World Series victory since 1933 while winning the batting title.

The signings of Robinson, Irvin, and Mays helped the National League corner the market on great black players for more than a generation. The American League lagged far behind. Its first black superstar did not appear until the late 1960s when Reggie Jackson joined the Oakland A's, twenty years after Robinson had broken the color barrier. In the 1950s such stars as Ernie Banks, Hank Aaron, Frank Robinson, and Curt Flood helped the senior circuit pull even and then ahead of the American League as measured by All-Star Game victories and World Series triumphs. When Robinson entered the majors, the American League had a record of 9 wins and 4 losses in All-Star contests. Over the next generation the National League reversed that figure, winning 11 and losing 6. Black players contributed to these victories, particularly Mays, who shined in the mid-season classics.

In the World Series the American League edge was largely the work of the New York Yankees, who since the late 1920s had dominated post-season play. In the 1950s the two leagues divided ten World Series while in the 1960s the National League, with blacks such as Maury Wills, Bob Gibson, and Lou Brock making major contributions, won six world championships.

Despite its conservative nature, baseball did a commendable job of integrating the game in the 1950s and 1960s. If one compares the record of professional baseball on integration by the early 1960s with that of any other area of American life, the National Game acquits itself well. Certainly business, industry, the churches, universities, or the media hadn't made comparable strides in blending a formerly isolated minority into its midst. By 1959, a generation after Robinson integrated baseball, blacks were represented on every team in the major leagues. In 1961 major league rosters included sixty-four black players, or 14.5 percent of the total at a time when the black population of the nation was 10.5 percent. In few other areas of American life were blacks as well represented at that time.

The nagging concern for major league baseball in these years was not integration but the overwhelming domination of one city, New York. Between 1949 and 1956 the New York Yankees won seven pennants and six world championships while Brooklyn won five pennants and one World Series, and the Giants won two pennants and one world title. In those eight years only the Phillies in 1950 and Cleveland in 1954 broke the New York monopoly.

While not solely responsible for the attendance decline (television also played a major role), the lack of competition drove fans away from baseball. After peaking at 20.8 million fans in 1948, attendance declined five straight years to 14.4 million, a drop of more than 31 percent. Baseball attendance would not recover to 1948 levels until 1962 when four new teams entered the major leagues.

For some teams the decline at the gate defied explanation. The Brooklyn Dodgers, in pennant races every season from 1949, saw their attendance drop sharply. In 1952 a fine Dodger team won the pennant and took the Yankees to seven games in a well-played World Series. Yet that season the Dodgers drew just 1.1 million fans, a decline of 700,000 from 1947. Despite winning the pennant and World Series in 1954, the Giants saw their attendance fall by almost half a million from its peak. Something clearly was wrong.

In retrospect it appears that a combination of factors had created a quiet crisis for professional baseball. Lack of competition among the franchises was an obvious problem. And the spread of television, from an infant industry in the late

1940s to a giant by the mid-1950s, created a nightmare for the baseball establishment. In 1947 there were approximately twenty thousand TV sets in use throughout the nation. Ten years later the figure was 40 million. Almost 70 percent of American homes had one. The men who ran baseball did not understand the new medium and reacted with the same obtuseness they had displayed in first confronting radio. They could not understand how to use this new medium to their advantage and spread baseball's popularity. Branch Rickey, usually an innovator, feared television. Radio created interest among fans, he argued, while television satiated them. In the 1950s almost every team signed lucrative television deals that increased their revenues while believing that the medium was keeping fans at home. As baseball discovered in the 1970s, television can create fan interest. What the televising of major league games in fact did was to undermine the minor leagues. Minor league attendance, which had grown from 15 million in 1946 to 42 million three years later, by 1960 had dropped to 10 million. As fans watched major leaguers on television, minor league attendance plummeted all through the 1950s.

Another factor in the decline of baseball attendance—and a major one in many cases—was the location of the ballparks. With the exception of Municipal Stadium in Cleveland, every major league park in use in the 1950s had been built between 1909 and 1923. By the mid-fifties their neighborhoods had declined, beset with racial problems and no longer convenient for preferred automobile transportation. Ebbets Field, for example, had parking for just seven hundred cars, Shibe Park for a thousand. At the turn of the century, the black population in the original eleven cities with baseball franchises had been minuscule: 1.9 percent in New York, 2 percent in Chicago, 1.2 percent in Detroit, and 5 percent in Philadelphia. By the 1950s these percentages had risen sharply as the result of the black migration north during two world wars. According to the 1960 census, the black population of New York was now 14 percent, of Chicago 23 percent, and of both Detroit and Philadelphia 29 percent. These populations were concentrated in the older sections of the cities, precisely where the ballparks had been built.

After World War II major league baseball found itself in the same area of the country, the Northeast and Midwest, where the game had been founded at the turn of the century. Meanwhile the fastest-growing areas in the nation were the West and the South. Expansion made sense.

## California Dreaming

JUST BEFORE World War II the St. Louis Browns seriously considered moving to Los Angeles. But the war ended that possibility, given the overloaded state of transportation at the time. Scattered discussions of franchise relocations arose after the war, but the prosperity of those years effectively silenced it. In the early 1950s the issue resurfaced as at least half a dozen franchises began to suffer from declining attendance, old ballparks, and poor urban locations.

The logjam was broken after the 1952 season by the Boston Braves. Always a weak franchise and second in popularity in Boston to the Red Sox, the Braves under the leadership of a new owner, the construction magnate Lou Perini, and an excellent general manager, John Quinn, had become a successful team in the late 1940s. They won the pennant in 1948, attracting more than 1.5 million fans. But from that point they couldn't compete with Ted Williams and the Red Sox. A couple of poor finishes left them in 1952 in seventh place, drawing just 281,000 fans. The Red Sox meanwhile were still able to attract more than a million fans a season. It was obvious that Boston could not sustain two teams and that the Red Sox held the loyalty of New England fans.

During spring training in 1953, Perini secured the permission of other National League clubs to move the Braves to Milwaukee. Milwaukee's population base was only 630,000 at the time, but the upper Midwest was baseball mad and an untapped territory. The area enthusiastically supported a minor league team in the early 1940s, run with his usual flair by Bill Veeck. Milwaukee fans took the Braves to their hearts, much in the way Brooklyn embraced its beloved Bums. Braves' players were showered with gifts of food and free car rentals, and were bewildered by the generosity of the fans. Over the next seven years the Braves' attendance averaged 2 million per year. The team won back-to-back pennants in 1957 and 1958 and the World Series in 1957 with a solid club built around such future Hall of Famers as Eddie Mathews, Warren Spahn, and Henry Aaron.

The Braves' success in Milwaukee opened the way for more franchise moves. In 1953 the pathetic Browns, no longer capable of competing in St. Louis against a Cardinal team owned by the Busch family (of Budweiser beer), moved to Baltimore. Their move was approved only when Bill Veeck had divested himself of the Browns. The Lords of Baseball were not about to let the despised Veeck cash in on a potentially rich baseball environment.

The Browns' move proved to be less successful than the Braves', largely because the Browns were a bad team. The novelty of major league baseball in Baltimore soon faded. Baltimore did not embrace baseball until the end of the 1950s, when Paul Richards built a dynasty of "Baby Birds" to challenge the Yankees for American League domination.

In 1954 the cash-poor Philadelphia Athletics pulled up

stakes for Kansas City in one of the poorest-planned franchise moves. The A's had fallen in the affections of the Philadelphia fans after the success of the Phillies' Whiz Kids. The A's organization could not compete with the DuPont money that backed the Phillies and was poorly run by Connie Mack's two sons, Roy and Earle—of whom it was said, "The sons became senile before their father." The deal to move to Kansas City was organized by a financial wheeler-dealer named Arnold Johnson, who was suspected with some justification of being a cat's paw for the New York Yankees. (Kansas City had been the Yankees' leading farm club.)

Kansas City was not a major league town in the mid-1950s and the A's, like the Browns, were a terrible team. They had little success in the Midwest and in 1967 moved west to Oakland, California.

These first franchise moves in fifty years were largely cosmetic and had not dealt with the nation's changing demographics. Baltimore, Milwaukee, and Kansas City had held major league franchises in the past. They also were within the geographic area where major league baseball was first established. The real opportunity lay in California, the fastest-growing state in the nation. By 1957 jet travel made transcontinental flights practical. It was only a question of time before some baseball entrepreneur would begin to mine the golden West. Walter O'Malley of the Dodgers turned out to be that man.

O'Malley is one of the most maligned figures in modern baseball, a difficult man to like. He had taken over the Dodgers in 1950 by ousting Branch Rickey from control. Unlike Rickey he was not a baseball man, but he was shrewd about the business side of baseball. He saw the implications of the Braves' move to Milwaukee: they were outdrawing the Dodgers by almost 2 to 1. Over time the Braves would have more money available to develop baseball talent, and the Dodgers would fall steadily behind them.

The Negro leagues, which the Dodgers had successfully exploited, were gone; now scouting and player development would determine which team signed the black talent. By the mid-1950s the Dodger edge dating back to Jackie Robinson was gone. O'Malley saw drastic measures were necessary if the Dodgers were to continue as a baseball powerhouse.

He regarded Ebbets Field with its limited seating, declining neighborhood, and lack of parking as outdated. Initially he talked of relocating the Dodgers in Brooklyn, at a confluence of subway, trolley, and bus lines. He would arrange to build the ballpark and would keep the concessions, and the city or state would supply the land. But O'Malley's plans brought him into conflict with one of New York's great power brokers, Robert Moses. Moses' power was based on his position on various state and city authorities such as the Triborough Bridge Commission and the City Commission of New York City with special powers over the Parks Department. Mayors and governors bowed to his political influence. Moses regarded the Dodgers' plan as not only too costly but also probably illegal because it involved government-controlled land. As an alternative, Moses suggested moving the team to Flushing Meadows, site of the 1939 World's Fair. O'Malley refused to bite because he knew that the new ballpark would be state-built and he would thus lose full control of the team's finances.

While O'Malley was squabbling with New York city and state authorities, Los Angeles mayor Norris Poulson was working hard to lure a team west. So was the mayor of San Francisco, the politically well-connected George Christopher. In 1956 and 1957 New York thought it had time to work out a way of keeping the Dodgers and Giants, but in the end California wanted them more than New York.

San Francisco approached Giants' owner Horace Stoneham in 1957 with an offer he could not turn down: a $5 million bond issue to build a new stadium with seating for 40,000 and parking for 10,000 to 12,000 cars. The Giants were guaranteed a profit of $200,000 to $250,000 a year versus the $81,000 they had earned in 1956. Contrary to myth, it was the Giants, not the Dodgers, who left New York first. On August 19 Stoneham called a press conference to break the news. "We're sorry to disappoint the kids of New York," he said, "but we didn't see many of their parents out there at the Polo Grounds in recent years."

O'Malley followed the trail west shortly after the end of the 1957 season. He had bought the minor league park Wrigley Field in Los Angeles and the Cubs' franchise there from Phil Wrigley, thus giving the Dodgers rights to the city. Mayor Poulson made him a lucrative offer. The authorities would supply the Dodgers with land in the city, most likely in the Chavez Ravine section, plus a guarantee to upgrade road access. In return O'Malley would build his own ballpark. On October 8 the Dodgers voted to move west. A half-century of National League baseball in New York came to a sad and inglorious end.

The press and public demanded explanations. O'Malley, with his fat face, sleek hair, and perpetual cigar, was an easy villain: his greed had cost Brooklyn its beloved Bums. But in fact the Dodgers and Giants were acting the way baseball teams had historically behaved—searching for greater profits. The New York political establishment had only itself to blame. Governor Averell Harriman had no interest in sport, and Mayor Robert Wagner of New York deferred to Moses, who thought he had O'Malley over a barrel. There were plenty of bunglers but only one victim, the loyal fans of the Dodgers and Giants.

On the other hand, the move west was overdue. Baseball could not neglect the potential wealth of the West Coast. No one could deny the success of the Giants and Dodgers over the next few years. Two teams who had seen attendance gradually decline in New York found themselves in the midst of a baseball boom in California. In their last three years in New York these two teams had drawn 5.3 million fans. In their first three years on the West Coast they drew 10.6 million.

Largely because of the move to California, major league baseball seemed healthy in the last years of the Eisenhower era. Attendance rose steadily through the end of the decade, and in 1960 the major leagues attracted almost twenty million fans, their best performance since 1949. Another sign of vitality was the fact that in 1958, 1959, and 1960 three different teams, the Braves, Dodgers, and Pirates, won pennants in the National League. The Yankees' monopoly in the junior circuit was broken in 1959 when a Chicago White Sox team, nicknamed the Go-Go Sox, easily ousted them for the pennant.

The first wave of great Latin players began to appear in the late 1950s, forerunners of a group who would help transform baseball in the next decades. Led by Minnie Minoso, the dynamic Cuban outfielder with Cleveland and Chicago, and Luis Aparicio, the best shortstop of his era and the individual who revived base running as an integral part of the game for the first time in more than fifty years, Latin talent became a part of almost every team. The Giants were among the most successful in developing this new area of player riches. Orlando Cepeda and Felipe Alou broke in with them in 1958, and Juan Marichal in 1960. Roberto Clemente first made the Pirates in 1955 as a twenty-one-year-old but didn't have his first great year until 1960 when he helped lead Pittsburgh to its first pennant in thirty-three years. By 1960 the rosters of most major league teams were dotted with Latin players, many of them—such as Tony Taylor and Tony Gonzalez of the Phillies, Chico Fernandez of the Detroit Tigers, and Pedro Ramos and Camilo Pascual of the Senators—solid players. Unlike the emphasis on black talent by the National League, Latin players were developed by teams in both leagues.

As the 1950s ended, major league baseball seemed poised for another prosperous era. It had completed the integration of the game, presided over the first franchise moves in fifty years, made tentative efforts to deal with the new medium of television, and begun the integration of Latin players, all major accomplishments. New challenges awaited.

*The "Miracle Mets" win the 1969 World Series.*

# Chapter 8

# COMING APART, 1961–1977

THE UNITED STATES entered the 1960s with a growing sense of optimism. A new administration led by John Fitzgerald Kennedy, the youngest president since Teddy Roosevelt, replaced the oldest president in American history, the grandfatherly Dwight Eisenhower. Kennedy set the tone for his presidency with his promises to "get the country moving again," forge a "New Frontier," and land a man on the moon before the end of the decade. With his beautiful young wife and handsome family, Kennedy captured the nation's imagination. While his performance never matched his rhetoric, Kennedy created a new style for the presidency, the president as celebrity.

The postwar economic boom continued unabated, reaching new levels in the years between 1961 and 1967. The nation's gross national product rose from $475 billion to $650 billion in these years while unemployment remained low and inflation was held to an insignificant 3 percent. A gigantic interstate highway system, launched under Eisenhower, fed the suburban housing boom of these years. In 1967 automobile sales reached a remarkable 9.3 million units.

America seemed dynamic and alive in the 1960s as the first of the Baby Boom generation entered high school. But problems largely neglected during the Eisenhower era continued to simmer. Racial segregation, cold war fears of a nuclear holocaust, and the problem of poverty amidst plenty soon began to play on the American conscience.

Major league baseball shared in the nation's prosperity and optimism. In 1960 the threat of a third major league, the Continental League, forced the majors to expand for the first time since 1901. The Continental League was Branch Rickey's last beau geste, an attempt to revitalize baseball by creating real competition with the two major leagues. Rickey forgot the record of past failures such as the Players League, the Federal League, and the Mexican League in his enthusiasm to challenge the baseball establishment. In 1961 the American League began the expansion process by adding two new teams, in Los Angeles and Washington, D.C., while the old Senators franchise moved to the twin cities of Minneapolis–St. Paul. The senior circuit followed the next year by granting franchises to the New York Metropolitans, soon called the Mets, and the Houston Colt 45s, known after 1964 as the Astros because of Houston's connection to the space program.

The National League got the best of this bargain. It returned baseball to New York where in the Dodgers' and Giants' last year the two teams had drawn 1.6 million fans between them. In the Big Apple there was a clear market for National League baseball. The move to Texas also opened the rich Southwest to baseball. In their first season in the majors the two new National League franchises drew more than 1.8 million fans, 600,000 more than the two new American League teams.

The Mets in particular became enormously popular,

partly because of their location in America's biggest media market and partly due to their incredible ineptitude—the team lost a record 120 games in its first season. The Mets' owners shrewdly brought Casey Stengel back to manage in New York. With his wit, Stengel helped humanize the Mets' incompetence. "Can't anyone here play the game?" he would moan as the Mets committed another baseball atrocity. But the New York press loved him and his team.

The American League's franchise choices were a mistake. The new Senators franchise failed to develop a following in the nation's capital and in 1977 moved to Texas. The Los Angeles Angels, owned by cowboy movie star and media mogul Gene Autry, fared better. The organization was run by shrewd baseball people such as former Braves manager Fred Haney, who was Autry's general manager, and Bill Rigney, who was named field manager. The Angels won seventy games in their first season, a record for a first-year team.

But Autry's situation was scarcely a happy one. He had to pay an indemnity of $325,000 to play in a town where league rights were owned by the Dodgers. When Walter O'Malley opened Dodger Stadium in 1962, the Angels became his tenant at a prohibitive price. Eventually Autry moved the Angels south to Orange County and changed their name to the California Angels (later the Anaheim Angels). They became the first major league franchise based in a suburb, but they failed to duplicate the success of O'Malley's Dodgers.

These years also saw major league baseball expand beyond U.S. borders for the first time, establishing teams first in Montreal in 1969 and then in Toronto eight years later. Neither Canadian team was a great initial success on the field or with fans, but the moves demonstrated that baseball was thinking beyond its origins.

In 1969, in order to deal with the problems of a twelve-team league, baseball decided to create two divisions of six teams for each major league. Baseball's experience with a twelve-team league in the late 1890s hadn't been positive and had contributed to the creation of the American League at the turn of the century. Two divisions of six teams each demanded a playoff to determine a league pennant winner. The best-of-five division playoffs that began in 1969 were not successful at first but by the mid-1970s were accepted by fans and provided exciting baseball.

With all its flaws, baseball's expansion and reorganization paid dividends. Attendance rose from 18.9 million in 1961 to more than 38.7 million sixteen years later. Total attendance for the 1960s decade was 231 million, an increase of 63 million over the preceding decade. The 2 million figure for a single team, which had been surpassed only seven times before 1961 and all in the American League, was now reached twenty-nine times, mostly in the National League. After moving into their new stadium in 1962, the Dodgers routinely drew 2 million-plus fans. In 1977 they missed the 3 million mark by less than 45,000. The Phillies, Cincinnati, St. Louis, New York, Houston, and even Atlanta in the senior circuit topped the 2 million mark during these years.

Along with expansion, a burst of stadium building fueled this baseball boom. Ten of the twelve teams in the National League moved into new "multi-purpose" stadiums in the generation after expansion in 1962, while five new parks were built in the American League. These multi-purpose grotesqueries soon were seen as disasters. They were too large for baseball, usually seating more than sixty thousand fans, and were so uniformly designed that it was difficult to tell one from another. They were built with public money and often controlled by a semi-governmental body and not by the teams. Located on the fringe of the city or in a nearby suburb, they were designed to take advantage of the new freeways that crisscrossed the country. The proliferation of these new stadiums explains why the National League outdrew the American League every year from 1962 to 1977, when new teams in Seattle and Toronto pushed the American League ahead.

On the field, one significant consequence of expansion was a dilution of talent, a problem that had been brewing for some time. Baseball clearly had been the most popular sport in America since the organization of professional sports in the late nineteenth century, but the 1960s saw the first serious challenge to its popularity. College and professional football, then professional basketball won large followings among young men.

College football boomed after World War II, especially as the game proved highly suitable to the new medium of television. Notre Dame with its national following of "subway alumni," Ohio State under Woody Hayes, the University of Alabama led by Bear Bryant—all became sports powerhouses with a following broader than their school's alumni.

Professional football received a huge boost in 1958 from an exciting, nationally televised championship game between the Baltimore Colts and the New York Giants. In the early 1960s television embraced pro football in a major way with Sunday telecasts over the CBS network. In 1960 the founding of a rival league, The American Football Conference (AFC), further boosted the sport, especially when the ABC network began televising games in competition with CBS. The advent of "Monday Night Football" in 1970, developed by Roone Arledge, clinched ABC's dominance in sports broadcasting.

The success of Vince Lombardi's Green Bay Packers in the mid-1960s was instrumental in popularizing pro football. His philosophy of "winning isn't everything, it's the only thing" captured the nation's mood. Green Bay became America's team despite Dallas's later claim to that distinction. In 1964 the rival AFC signed quarterback Joe Namath for the incredible sum of $427,000 to play for the New York Jets, giving the new league its first superstar and a figure whose flair and anti-establishment aura charmed the nation's youth.

Another factor in the emergence of professional football was the development of a championship game between the two leagues. Christened the Super Bowl and staged on a Sunday in January, the game soon attracted huge audiences and became the most successful of the playoff formats. By the 1970s football had become the most popular sport on television.

The rise of professional basketball in the 1960s was a further warning signal for baseball. Pro basketball has been around for years, but its following was small. In the late 1950s talented blacks who might earlier have chosen to play baseball began to monopolize basketball. Around 1962–1963 the best black players began to have an impact on pro basketball. The flashy style of play formerly seen only in Harlem Globetrotters exhibitions now became part of the pro game. Teams such as the Boston Celtics, with its great black defensive star Bill Russell; the Philadelphia Warriors, led by Wilt Chamberlain, who revolutionized basketball scoring records; and the Los Angeles Lakers, whose star player was the exciting Elgin Baylor, brought a new level of enthusiasm to basketball. These players opened up the game, and in the process fans discovered a new national sport.

Not only was baseball losing the black talent to these rival sports, but the game itself now seemed to lack the kind of flashy, exciting superstars that football and basketball regularly produced. Mickey Mantle retired in 1968, Willie Mays suddenly was no longer the "Say Hey Kid" but a tired old man, and Hank Aaron, the greatest hitter of his generation, lacked the charisma of a Babe Ruth, Joe DiMaggio, or Ted Williams. Aaron generated excitement in the early 1970s as he pursued and broke Babe Ruth's all-time home run record of 714, finishing with 755 for his career. But Aaron never was a big drawing card in the way past superstars had been. Despite its success at the box office, baseball was drifting toward troubled times.

The loss of black talent was somewhat offset by baseball's greater reliance on Latin players, who in the 1960s made their greatest impact. During the decade virtually every major league team could count good Latin players on its roster. Roberto Clemente of the Pirates, the forerunner of this Latin breakthrough, in the 1960s won four batting titles. After winning in 1964 and 1965, he lost the batting championship to a fellow Latin, Matty Alou in 1966, before winning again the next season. Tony Oliva won the batting championships in his first two years in the American League, 1964–1965. Oliva might have become one of the greatest hitters in history but for a series of knee injuries that shortened his career.

Orlando Cepeda won two RBI titles, one with the Giants in 1961 and a second with the Cardinals six years later. Among other successful Latin players were Camilo Pascual, who twice led the American League in strikeouts and once in victories; Zoilo Versalles, who led the Minnesota Twins to a pennant in 1965 and was named the American League's MVP; and future Hall of Famer Juan Marichal, the decade's winningest pitcher. Marichal led the National League in victories in 1963 and 1968 and earned run average in 1969.

Unfortunately for baseball, one of the greatest sources of Latin talent, Cuba, was lost in the early 1960s after the break in relations with the United States brought on by the rise of Fidel Castro. The main suppliers of Latin American players became Puerto Rico and the Dominican Republic while

Venezuela and Panama contributed a handful of talented players. No single team dominated the signing of Latin players as the Dodgers had with blacks, but the Giants and Twins were among the most successful. By the end of the decade every major league organization was scouting the Caribbean.

In addition to the loss of black talent to rival sports, professional baseball in the late 1960s was regarded as conservative and out of touch with the social changes sweeping the nation. Mike Burke, president of the Yankees, speaking in 1968 saw the danger in baseball's isolation from young people who preferred contact sports such as football, basketball, and hockey. What was needed, he argued was "strong, courageous, intelligent leadership." Instead the baseball establishment floundered.

The game was slow to add minority executives to its front office, and those who were chosen often smacked of tokenism. In the late 1960s Jesse Owens, the great Olympic champ, was made baseball's troubleshooter to improve race relations. By that time Owens had little validity in the black community. It was an indictment of baseball that they had to turn to an outsider to improve race relations while neglecting someone like Jackie Robinson who was still seen as a hero to many young blacks. Only in 1968 did baseball hire Monte Irvin as an assistant to the commissioner with a special interest in racial matters. Irvin eventually did a good job in public relations, but his position at least in the beginning was a form of window dressing.

## Changes in the Game

ONE OF baseball's major problems in the generation after expansion was a decline in hitting as reflected in lower batting averages, an enormous increase in strikeouts, and the dominance of pitching. In 1963 the strike zone was broadened. Together with higher mounds in the newer ballparks, this provided pitchers with a significant advantage. Between 1963 and 1967 the earned run average in both leagues was around 3.50, lower on average by half a run from the preceding decade. In 1968 both leagues' earned run averages dropped below 3.00, to 2.98 for the American League and 2.99 for the National. The last time a major league season had seen that low an ERA was 1919, before Babe Ruth launched the age of the long ball.

One statistic that brings the domination of pitching into clear relief is the number of shutouts recorded. In the last year before the mound was raised (1962), the National League recorded 95 shutouts; six years later that figure had risen to 185. The total for both leagues was an incredible 345. With the lowering of the mound in 1969 the shutout total dropped to 239.

In 1968 Denny McLain of the Tigers became the first pitcher since Dizzy Dean in 1934 to win 30 games. That same year Bob Gibson of the Cardinals compiled a remarkable earned run average of 1.12, plus 13 shutouts, figures not seen since the Dead Ball days. The American League ERA leader was Luis Tiant with 1.40 while five starters had earned run averages of under 2.00. Ten pitchers in both leagues struck out 200 or more batters that season.

In the 1960s pitching dominance reached pre-1920 levels and produced astounding records. When he first entered the major leagues, the Dodgers' Sandy Koufax combined wildness with overpowering speed and a devastating curve, but his record between 1955 and 1960 was just 36 wins and 48 losses. Beginning in 1961, as he mastered control, his record over the next seven seasons was among the greatest in baseball history:

129 wins against 47 losses. During this time he struck out 300 batters in three seasons, had an earned run average under 2.00 three times, and threw four no-hit games. In four World Series his ERA was 0.95 while striking out 61 batters in 57 innings.

Joining Koufax as dominant pitchers in this era were Bob Gibson of the Cardinals and Juan Marichal of the Giants. Gibson came into his own in 1961 and won 184 games during the decade. He struck out 200 or more for eight years and would have made it nine but for a broken leg midway through the 1967 season. During the decade he won 20 games four times and 19 once.

Marichal wasn't far behind Koufax and Gibson in effectiveness. He won 207 games during the decade, struck out more than 200 six times, and won 25 or more games three different times.

The American League had no pitchers as consistently successful as this threesome but Jim Kaat, "Sudden" Sam McDowell, and Denny McLain posted impressive records. On his way to winning 283 games, Kaat came into his own in 1962 and helped Minnesota to win a division championship and a league pennant. He won 25 games in 1966, tying Whitey Ford who also won 25 in 1961 for the most wins in the American League since 1946 when Bob Feller and Hal Newhouser reached that figure.

McDowell had an overpowering fastball that enabled him twice between 1965 and 1970 to strike out more than 300 batters. He never became a polished pitcher because of poor work habits and a drinking problem that shortened his career. For a handful of seasons, however, he was one of the most feared pitchers in baseball.

McLain may have been the most talented of the lot. At age 21 he won 16 games. Between 1965 and 1969 he won 108 games including 31 wins in 1968 and 24 the next season. But

he was an uncontrollable egomaniac whom no one could disci-
pline. Eventually he hurt his arm, got into trouble for gambling, and was finished as a top pitcher at 25. He later wound
up in jail for drug dealing and various con games.

Adding to the dominance of pitching in this era was
the proliferation of great relief pitchers. The relief specialist
had been around baseball for years, but only in the late
1950s and early 1960s did it become imperative for a pennant-
contending team to have someone to come out of the bullpen
and shut down the opposition. In the past the relief pitcher
had been either a starter pressed into emergency service or an
older pitcher finishing his career. There were a few excep-
tions—Hugh Casey for the Dodgers in the 1940s, Joe Page for
two magnificent seasons for the Yankees in the late 1940s, and
Ellis Kinder of the Red Sox, who moved from starter to reliever while he was at the peak of his game.

Page and Kinder had set the record for most saves, 27, in
1949 and 1954 respectively. That figure went unchallenged
until the 1960s when it was shattered almost yearly as different standards for the save rule were developed. Luis Arroyo
saved 29 games for the Yankees in 1961, four years later the 30
mark was broken by journeyman pitcher Ted Abernathy of
the Cubs. Between 1965 and 1977 the 30 mark was bettered
thirteen times, with John Hiller of the Tigers setting the save
record in 1973 at 38.

An examination of the pennant or division winners
makes it clear that having a dominant reliever was crucial to a
team's success. Between 1961 and 1977 the league leader in
saves pitched for pennant or division winners nine times in the
American League and eight times in the National League.

In effect, the rise of the relief pitcher meant that batters
could no longer count on facing a tired starter or a second-
string pitcher late in the game. Instead, with the game on the

line batters would now be confronted with a pitcher who for one or two innings was as overpowering or dominant as the best starter. Stan Musial once observed that the emergence of the relief specialist was one of the greatest changes in baseball during his career.

As a result, hitting levels dropped to a fifty-year low. The batting champ in the American League in 1968, Carl Yastrzemski, hit .301 and was the *only* batter to break the .300 mark. A total of just three men in both leagues managed to achieve 300 or more total bases. The National League saw just 891 homers hit in 1968, the lowest figure since 1954. The home run total of 1,895 for both leagues in 1968 was down almost 60 percent from 1962. That year attendance declined by 1.2 million fans.

In a desperate attempt to inject offense into the game and revive fan interest, in 1973 American League owners unanimously voted to adopt a "designated hitter" (DH) rule. An offensive hitter would regularly bat for the pitcher but would not play in the field. This idea had been kicking around baseball for years. It had been given serious consideration in 1928 when National League president John Heydler proposed it as a way for the senior circuit to match the more popular American League led by homer-hitting Babe Ruth.

In 1972 the American League consistently lagged behind the National League in most offensive categories, reversing a trend dating back to Ruth. One consequence was that the National League was outdrawing the junior circuit by a substantial margin. In 1972 the American League's attendance was just 74 percent of the National's, a worrisome trend.

The introduction of the designated hitter may have offended baseball purists, but it did succeed in raising batting averages. In 1969 the National League had hit .243; in the American League the figure was an astounding .230, the lowest in league history. Even in 1908, the year of Chicago's "Hitless Wonders," the American League had hit for a .239 average.

In its first year the DH rule raised the American League average by 20 points, to .259. Over the next few years it enabled the league consistently to outhit the senior circuit. Attendance began to rise at the same time, though it still lagged behind the National League until 1977 when the American League added two new teams.

Some of baseball's troubles could also be traced to the end of the Yankee era of domination. From 1921 to 1964 the Yankees had been the most successful team in major league baseball, if not in all sports. They won 29 pennants and 20 World Series in that period, including five consecutive pennants between 1960 and 1964. But the superb organization that made shrewd trades began to unravel, and the excellent farm system that supplied fresh talent began to dry up. The Yankee team that won 99 games and took the Cardinals to seven games in the 1964 World Series before losing was showing signs of age. Mickey Mantle was 33, Elston Howard was 35, and Roger Maris, Tony Kubek, and Whitey Ford were suffering from injuries. In 1964 Del Webb and Dan Topping sold the most successful franchise in baseball to CBS for $14.2 million, the highest purchase price of any sports franchise to that date. Topping and Webb said they were willing to sell only because they believed that CBS would maintain the Yankees' high standards. "CBS has earned such a place in radio and television," they wrote. "We believe CBS' association with the Yankees will be good for baseball, for sports generally and for the public." If there were any doubts about the intrusion of television into baseball, the CBS deal ended that. Television would increasingly dictate baseball's future.

CBS thought it got a bargain but found out instead that

it had bought a declining franchise whose talented minor league system was drying up. The team needed an infusion of new blood to continue to compete, but the best player in the Yankees' minor league organization in 1965 was Roger Repoz, a far cry from Lou Gehrig, Joe DiMaggio, or Mickey Mantle. In 2,100 times at bat during his career, Repoz managed to hit just .224, the lowest average of any outfielder in baseball history with that length of career.

Mantle hung on for four more years but never again hit more than 30 home runs or drove in more than 56 runs in a season. Maris was finished as a full-time player and in 1967 was traded to the Cardinals. Ford developed arm problems after the 1965 season and retired two years later.

The end of the Yankees dynasty was viewed as good for baseball because it would lead to greater balance in the American League. For the first time since World War II three different teams in three years won American League pennants: Minnesota (1965), Baltimore (1966), and Detroit (1967). But the fall of the Yankees took something out of baseball, even if only a team or franchise that fans could hate. In the long run the Yankee collapse did not provide better competition. From 1966 to 1970 the Baltimore Orioles dominated the league, then gave way to a great Oakland Athletics team put together by the shrewd baseball hustler Charles O. Finley. Between 1969 and 1975 Oakland averaged 93 victories and won five division titles, four pennants, and three World Series behind such great players as Reggie Jackson, Sal Bando, Jim "Catfish" Hunter, and Rollie Fingers.

During these years the competitive balance was better in the National League. No team dominated the way the Yankees had or even as effectively as Oakland in the early 1970s. Between 1961 and 1977 five different teams won pennants in the senior circuit. Between 1970 and 1977 Cincinnati and the

Pirates were the two best teams, winning pennants or division titles five of the eight years. The Mets won in 1973, the Dodgers the next year to break the Pirate-Reds monopoly.

Another characteristic of baseball in this era was the return to prominence of the stolen base for the first time since the Dead Ball era. Luis Aparicio had revived base-stealing in the late 1950s; in the early 1960s Maury Wills of the Dodgers ran at every opportunity. In 1962 he shattered Ty Cobb's seemingly unbreakable record of 96 stolen bases in one season by pilfering 104. Twelve years later Lou Brock of the Cardinals broke Wills's mark by stealing 118 bases.

The effect on the game of a revival in base-stealing is not as clear as the importance of relief pitching. Oakland led the American League with 341 steals in 1976, but finished in second place. In 1964 the total number of stolen bases in both leagues was 1,176; twelve years later that figure had swollen to 3,054, but with no correlation to the winning of pennants or World Series. Between 1961 and 1977 only seven World Series winners led their league in stealing bases. Few pennant winners or World Series champs could claim the league's stolen-base leader. The Dodgers with Maury Wills and the Cardinals with Lou Brock got mileage out of the running game, but they were the exception, not the rule. The stolen base may have enlivened baseball, but it wasn't a major factor in determining the best team in the league.

## Enter Marvin Miller

BY 1966 the American political and social climate had undergone a dramatic change from the optimism of John F. Kennedy's early presidency. The war in Vietnam had begun to radicalize the nation, especially its draft-age young. Racial

strife spread out of the South into the ghettos of the big
Northern and Midwestern cities. A youth culture that featured alienation and fascination with drugs left the older generation confused and bewildered.

Baseball mirrored these developments as players in the
mid- to late 1960s became dissatisfied with the game's basic
agreement. There were early signs of trouble. Before the 1966
season, pitchers Sandy Koufax and Don Drysdale of the
Dodgers agreed to a joint holdout, something new. They
signed contracts at the end of spring training, and their deal—
contracts in excess of $100,000 each—showed other players
what collective action might achieve.

In 1966 the Major League Baseball Players Association
took a fateful decision that forever changed the game—it
hired Marvin Miller as chief spokesman. Miller, forty-eight,
had served for sixteen years as chief economist for the United
Steel Workers of America and since 1960 had been assistant to
the union's president. He knew his way around contentious
labor-management issues, but even he wasn't prepared for the
scope of baseball's labor problems.

The Players Association believed its previous spokesman,
Judge Robert Cannon of Wisconsin, should have been more
aggressive in protecting the players' interests. The Association
demonstrated its seriousness by giving Miller a two-year contract at $50,000 per year plus a $20,000 expense account. At
the time the average salary of a major league player was
around $19,000.

Miller was shocked by the conservatism of the players he
represented. Although occasionally irritated by the high-
handedness of the owners, the players generally saw them as
partners rather than adversaries. Miller realized that his first
task was to educate the players about their rights. He quickly
discovered that salaries were scandalously low. In 1966 rook-

ies received $6,000 while the average player earned $19,000 and only a handful of players made $100,000, a figure achieved by Joe DiMaggio and Ted Williams a generation earlier. Yet for most players the pension issue was more important. They regarded baseball as a transition to another career after their playing days were over. Major league baseball had created a solid pension system after World War II, but there were constant squabbles between players and owners over financing.

Miller decided that his first task was to win the confidence of the players. He did this quickly. When he discovered that they received a flat fee of $125 from Topps Chewing Gum for appearing on the company's bubble gum cards, Miller renegotiated the contract into a royalty arrangement. Then he signed an exclusive agreement for players to endorse Coca-Cola, with the revenues to be designated for the pension program. His breakthrough with the players came when he extracted a better players' contract from the owners.

The 1966 basic agreement increased the rookie salary to $10,000, strengthened the provisions for health insurance and widows' benefits, and created a new pension structure. A player with five years in the major leagues would receive a pension of $250 per month at 50 or $644 if he waited until age 65. The amount of the pension rose with years of service. A ten-year veteran would receive $500 at 50 and $1,288 at 65; a twenty-year man $600 and $1,488. No other sport, indeed, no other industry, could boast a better pension program. The pension issue continued to be the major concern of the players for a few more years and then gave way to arguments over salaries, freedom of movement, and eventually the abolition of the reserve clause.

Much of Miller's achievement was abetted by the stupidity and paternalism of the owners. They were used to treating the players as chattel or as children who had to be alternately disciplined or spoiled. They underestimated Miller's prowess and over the years committed serious blunders that cost them their control over baseball. They might have been saved by a strong, forward-looking commissioner, but when Miller appeared on the scene the commissioner's office was filled by General William Eckert, a man who admitted he knew nothing of baseball. Eckert, nicknamed Baseball's Unknown Soldier, was nothing more than a front man for the owners. When they fired him in 1969 they hired a lawyer with a baseball background, Bowie Kuhn. Kuhn would have made a great commissioner in the quieter 1940s or 1950s, but he was out of sync with the confrontational world of the 1970s. While Kuhn sincerely wanted the best for baseball and its players, he was consistently outmaneuvered by Miller or betrayed by the owners who had hired him.

Miller strengthened his position over the next few years as he fine-tuned the basic agreement. In 1972 he was able to lead a largely unified brief strike over various contract issues, in particular the players' demand for a huge increase in the pension plan. Miller's success in enlisting the players' support was evident from the fact that this difficult group of prima donnas voted 663 to 10 to endorse the strike.

Not everyone saw Miller in a positive light. Some older sportswriters such as Dick Young of the *New York Daily News* regarded him as a troublemaker while Bill Veeck, baseball's premier renegade, believed the union leader was bad for baseball. To Veeck, Miller was another typical labor boss who "to justify his existence . . . must always seek increases."

The 1972 players' strike was the turning point in baseball's labor relations history. It lasted thirteen days before the owners, not the union, caved in. The pension program was sweetened, but the most significant change in the 1973 contract provided for salary arbitration. Players with at least two years in the major leagues could choose to have their differences with ownership decided by an independent arbitrator. The owners accepted this concept without realizing its potential impact on salaries: the $19,000 average salary of 1967 grew to $46,000 eight years later.

Meanwhile the reserve clause became an issue again. After the 1969 season the Cardinals decided to revamp the team that had won pennants in 1967 and 1968 but had faltered badly that season. Among other moves, they traded center fielder Curt Flood and other players to the Phillies for slugging first baseman Richie Allen. It was an old-fashioned baseball deal, with one team unloading a troublemaker, Allen, while another tried to bring in a veteran player, Flood, to stabilize a group of younger players. At the time Flood was making $90,000 and was offered a $100,000 contract by the Phillies, later increased to $110,000. He refused to accept the deal and decided to sue baseball. "There ain't no way I'm going to pack up and move twelve years of my life away from here," Flood told reporters.

Miller cautioned Flood that in every test case the courts had upheld the reserve clause, giving the owners the right to trade players. Flood went ahead and eventually lost before the Supreme Court in a 5 to 3 decision written by Justice Harry Blackmun. Blackmun essentially repeated the arguments of earlier cases to the effect that with all its anomalies, the proper way to revise baseball was by legislative not judicial action.

Flood sat out a year, living in Europe, then in 1971 signed a contract for $110,000 to play with Bob Short's Washington Senators. After just thirteen games it was clear that he was finished. He left the club and took Short's entire $110,000 salary with him. Baseball had stiffed Flood; Flood stiffed Short.

The Flood case redirected attention to the inequities of the reserve clause at a time when both the nation's protest groups and its baseball players were growing more militant. In 1975 two players, Dave McNally of Montreal and Andy Messersmith of the Dodgers, decided to test the reserve clause from a different standpoint. Miller had noted that the standard players' contract bound the players for one year. But what if a player didn't sign a new contract while playing for his team that year—would he then become a free agent? Major league baseball said no, such a player would still be reserved to his team. But after the 1975 season, McNally and Messersmith appealed their case. Under the 1973 contract negotiated by Miller, the dispute eventually went to an arbitrator, in this case Peter Seitz, who ruled that the two players were free agents.

Seitz explained that he ruled as both a lawyer and an arbitrator. He wasn't striking a blow at the reserve clause, he said. "My own feeling is that the problems of the reserve system ought to be worked out by the parties in collective bargaining." Within minutes of his ruling, the owners fired Seitz, as was their right.

Seitz's decision revolutionized a century of labor-management relations in baseball. It meant that players could play out their contract and then sign with the team that made them the best offer. Miller counseled caution. He warned the players to use their newfound leverage carefully. Too many free agents could flood the market and drive down the players' bargaining position, an argument put forth by Charles Finley of the Oakland A's. Let everyone become a free agent, he said, and they would find their bargaining leverage feeble. Miller suddenly became a voice for moderation. When a new basic agreement was discussed after the 1976 season, he suggested creating a new format for players entering free agency.

The Players Association withdrew its demand for total free agency. A player now would be bound to his team for six years. Then he would be free to enter a special draft, eligible to be signed by any team. In return the owners agreed to boost the minimum salary to $21,000. Major league baseball was stepping into a new era without knowing what to expect. Would ticket prices skyrocket? Would a handful of wealthier teams monopolize the best players?

The first group of free agents did not dramatically change baseball's competitiveness. Of the four pennant winners in 1977, Los Angeles, Philadelphia, New York, and Kansas City, only the Yankees benefited from free agency. They had signed Reggie Jackson and pitcher Don Gullett before the season and both, especially Jackson, helped the Yankees win the pennant and the World Series. The other three teams had signed no free agents.

An analysis of the results of the first group of free agents showed if anything a waste of money. Some, such as pitcher Wayne Garland, who signed a ten-year, $1 million contract with Cleveland, were flops. Others, such as Sal Bando, Joe Rudi, Dave Cash, Bill Campbell, and Bert Campaneris, were either over the hill or just average players at this stage in their careers. Free agency showed simply that baseball management had to spend wisely and choose well. But it also illustrated that the rules of the baseball business were forever changed. It would take the owners years to learn that lesson.

*Marvin Miller, executive director of the Players Association, speaks with newsmen after rejecting a new proposal to end the 1981 baseball strike.*

## Chapter 9

# BEST OF TIMES, WORST OF TIMES, 1978–1994

THE MID-1970S were among the most difficult years in American history. The aftermath of the Vietnam War, with the United States ally South Vietnam being occupied by the forces of North Vietnam, left a sour feeling in America, a nation not accustomed to losing wars.

The collapse of the Nixon presidency in the Watergate scandal deepened feelings of anger, frustration, and mistrust of government. For the first time in U.S. history a president was forced to resign his office in disgrace.

These twin blows to America's pride were followed by the worst inflationary cycle in the nation's history. A gasoline shortage brought on by Middle East oil producers in 1973, then a second one in 1979, fueled the rise in prices and frayed the temper of a nation that depended on the automobile. Gasoline prices rose to unheard-of levels. Since the early fifties the United States had experienced relative price stability and real income growth. Beginning in the early 1970s the inflation rate rose steadily, reaching 12 percent in 1974 and 14 percent in 1980. Americans had not confronted serious inflation problems since the years immediately after World War II.

At the same time unemployment remained stubbornly high. Between 1976 and 1980 the rate never dropped below 5.8 percent and in 1977 reached 9 percent, a postwar high and a foreshadowing of the recession of 1981–1982 that drove the rate to double digits. Real income, which had grown steadily since 1945 for all groups in American society, slowed. In 1974 it actually fell. After the mid-1970s, only the top 40 percent of income earners showed improvement.

The United States was in the midst of traumatic transformation from a manufacturing to an information-based society. Jobs in heavy industry were disappearing; the old industrial Northeast and Midwest were transformed into the "Rust Belt" as population shifted to the South and West, the so-called Sun Belt. As the Baby Boom ended, the nation grew older, crankier, and more frustrated. Consensus liberalism, which had shaped the nation politically since FDR, was breaking apart.

By every measure America was adrift in the mid-1970s. It had lost confidence in itself and its future. Later President Jimmy Carter would refer to the nation as suffering from a crisis of spirit, what he referred to as a malaise. Baseball too had its sicknesses.

The years from 1978 to 1994 saw power and influence in baseball gradually pass from the owners, who had run the game from its origin, to the players. The undermining of the reserve clause, the growth of free agency, and the influence of arbitration on baseball salaries transformed the sport. Issues such as pension payments and the minimum salary disappeared as players discovered that their newfound bargaining power enabled them to command salaries previously reserved for entertainment superstars. The average salary of a baseball player rose from $121,000 in 1979 to more than $1.7 million by 1992—as recently as 1967 it had been just $19,000. According to the Associated Press, after the 1993 season 273 players made $1 million, 103 made $3 million, and 13 players received pay in excess of $5 million. That year Ryne Sandberg of the Cubs topped all players with a salary of $6,380,000, closely followed by two Mets, Bobby Bonilla at $6.2 million and Dwight Gooden at $6.1 million.

The owners struggled to regain control of "their" game, but they were consistently outmaneuvered by Marvin Miller and the Players Association. Management no longer had the special protection of the legal system. After their 1972 victory before the Supreme Court in the Curt Flood case, management lost whenever they turned to the courts.

In desperation they gradually adopted a more aggressive tone in their relations with the players. They agitated to dismiss Commissioner Bowie Kuhn, who was seen as having failed them when they lost control of the game in the mid-1970s. In 1976 Kuhn voided deals that Charles O. Finley had made to gain players and cash as he disbanded his Oakland dynasty. While there was no love for Finley in baseball circles, Kuhn's action threatened owners' prerogatives. What effectively finished Kuhn was baseball's worst strike yet, a work stoppage in 1981 that wiped out fifty days of the regular season and forced baseball to adopt a split-season format to determine pennant winners.

The 1981 strike grew out of the owners' determination to reverse the trend in baseball's labor relations. They sought to end the process of salary arbitration and change the rules pertaining to free agency so that a team losing a player would receive some kind of compensation. In professional football this so-called Rozelle rule (named after Commissioner Pete

Rozelle) had put an effective halt to the signing of free agents. In essence the baseball owners wished to be protected from their own foolishness. After all, they were the ones who were offering huge salaries to free agents.

When the Players Association refused to make concessions on these issues, the owners in 1980 voted to build a strike fund of close to $15 million and purchased insurance with Lloyd's of London to reimburse themselves in the event of a strike. Each club was to receive $1,150,000 if the strike lasted six weeks. The owners believed that the players would not be able to maintain their solidarity and that once the paychecks stopped the union would crack.

On June 10, 1981, negotiations between owners and the Players Association broke down. A strike followed that lasted exactly fifty days, the limit of the Lloyd's policy. More than seven hundred games were lost. The statistical sanctity of the baseball season, which had persisted with few changes since 1901, was destroyed. The deal that ended the strike in August 1981 was largely on the players' terms and would run for three years. It provided limited compensation for teams that lost certain star free agents, but arbitration was left unchanged. The 1981 contract was another victory for Marvin Miller and the Players Association, though the public tended to blame the players more than the owners for the mischief of the strike. The general manager of the Baltimore Orioles, Hank Peters, expressed the attitude of most baseball fans: "If we ever let it [a strike] happen again, kiss baseball goodbye." It would happen again, but baseball would somehow survive.

The animosity toward Miller on the part of the owners was so intense that it often blinded them to the successes of their game in the 1980s and the great profits each team was showing. The owners were out to get Miller at almost any cost.

Eventually their determination to wound him would cost them even more than the 1981 strike.

The strike came in the midst of an unusually exciting stretch of baseball play. Between 1978 and 1992 no team won consecutive World Series, and only two—Los Angeles and Minnesota—repeated during the fifteen-year period. It was the first time in baseball history that this kind of competitive balance had been achieved. Contrary to dire predictions, ending the reserve clause did not lead to a handful of wealthy teams signing the best players.

No dynasties appeared in the major leagues during these years to equal the great Yankee teams of the 1920s, 1930s, or 1950s, or even the 1949–1956 Dodgers. Because of the ease of player movement, it became difficult for any team to establish dominance in its league. Success went to those teams that spent wisely in the free-agent market but continued to develop talent in the minors. The New York Mets of the mid-1980s, for example, built a powerhouse around a few shrewd trades (Keith Hernandez, George Foster, and Gary Carter), while their first-class farm system funneled young talent such as Lenny Dykstra, Darryl Strawberry, and Dwight Gooden to the majors.

But the Mets began a precipitous decline in the early 1990s when they made a series of poor decisions relating to trades and free agency. They reached into the free-agent market and spent $6.2 million for Bobby Bonilla, a good but limited player who never blended into his team. They traded Lenny Dykstra—still young and a dynamic leadoff hitter— for Juan Samuel of the Phillies, who had proven he could not play any field position and had begun to slip offensively. At the same time the Mets' minor league system failed to produce. As a result the Mets' decline was as rapid as its rise. Player movement cut both ways.

Competitive balance in the 1980s led to a surge of interest in baseball. Attendance had reached the 40 million mark in 1978 and climbed above 43 million for the next two years. In the National League four teams—the Phillies, San Diego, Montreal, and Houston—set attendance records in these years. In the American League six teams set new attendance records: the Yankees, Texas Rangers, Boston Red Sox, California Angels, Kansas City Royals, and Milwaukee Brewers.

The attendance boom of the late 1970s was a preview of baseball's tremendous prosperity in the 1980s despite serious labor strife. In 1976 Bowie Kuhn negotiated a lucrative television agreement to play the World Series at night in order to reach a larger, prime-time audience. He also rescheduled the games so that a seven-game series would be spread over two weekends to maximize the audience. The concept was a success despite complaints by traditionalists that the World Series should be played in daytime. Television ratings indicated that the public enjoyed being able to watch the games in the evening. One of the most commonly voiced fears, that the games would be affected by cold weather, has not been an important factor in twenty-five years of World Series play at night.

In the mid-1980s a new commissioner, Peter Ueberroth, negotiated a lucrative television contract with CBS worth $1.08 billion. From it each team would receive more than $14 million a year, at the time a sum in excess of every team's payroll. At the same time every major league team continued to negotiate its own local television deal. By 1991 the New York Yankees received the most money of any team from local sources, $45 million per year. Seattle had the poorest deal at just $3 million per season. In the National League the biggest winners were the New York Mets at $24 million and the

Philadelphia Phillies at $21 million. The Pirates and Montreal each received just $6 million in local television revenues.

A by-product of this new prosperity was the rapid increase in the value of a baseball franchise. Since World War II the average price of a major league franchise had risen sharply. One estimate gives the increase as 100 percent in the 1950s, 87 percent in the 1960s, and 47 percent in the 1970s. For the 1980s the figure was 264 percent. The New York Mets, for example, sold for $21 million in 1980 and $100 million just six years later. The Baltimore Orioles went for $13 million in 1979 and $70 million nine years later. In 1992 the Seattle Mariners, not a particularly successful franchise, sold to a group of Japanese and American investors for a then-record price of $106 million. Overall the average price of a baseball franchise in the 1940s was around $2 million; a half-century later it had risen to more than $40 million.

In 1992, when the Florida Marlins and Colorado Rockies were added to the National League, the admission price (to be divided among the other teams) was $95 million, a considerable jump from the $2 million paid during the 1960s expansion of baseball. The expansion fee was divided as follows: each American League team received $3 million in return for making some players available for the new teams to draft. The remaining $142 million was divided among the twelve National League clubs, a one-time windfall of almost $12 million each. Both the Florida and Colorado teams were purchased by wealthy businessmen, Joseph Coors of Coors Beer in the case of the Rockies, and Wayne Huizenga of Blockbuster Video with the Marlins. This capped a powerful trend in the 1980s— the movement of business conglomerates into baseball ownership. During the 1980s Walter Haas, who manufactured Levis blue jeans, bought the Oakland A's; Tom Monaghan of

Domino's Pizza paid $53 million for the Detroit Tigers; and the Chicago Tribune Company purchased the Cubs from the Wrigley family. Major league baseball had always been big business, but in the 1980s it was becoming an investment bonanza.

## *The Game Within the Game*

BASEBALL in the generation after 1978 saw a continuation of trends that had first appeared in the 1960s: the growing influence of relief pitching, the dominance of power pitching as opposed to finesse, and a rise in home runs with a parallel increase in strikeouts.

Relief pitching had first asserted itself in the late 1950s but became an integral part of successful teams from the 1960s on. As the inimitable Yogi Berra put it, "If you ain't got a bullpen, you ain't got nothin'." In the 1970s a telltale statistic confirmed the impact of relief pitching: the number of complete games by starting pitchers began to decline. In 1972 Steve Carlton of the Phillies completed 30 games while three other pitchers had more than 20. The figures for the American League were comparable: four pitchers with 20 or more complete games. By the mid-1980s a total of 20 complete games was rare. Mario Soto of Cincinnati, for example, led the National League in 1984 with just 13. Four years later the National League had only three pitchers with more than 10 complete games. Teams now sought not just a dominant closer but also a deep bullpen which included "long relievers" and "set-up" men. Long men were pitchers who could come into the game and pitch three or four competent innings; set-up men prepared the way for the "closer," who now usually pitched just one inning.

The definition of a "save" by a relief pitcher has been modified a number of times since the 1970s, so that in the 1980s huge totals became commonplace. While 20 saves was once an impressive total, many closers began accumulating 30 or more saves in a single season. Soon the 50-save mark was reached. Between 1988 and 1992, while pitching for the Oakland A's, Dennis Eckersley averaged 44 saves, topped in 1992 by 51. Lee Smith of the St. Louis Cardinals saved 90 games over two seasons, 1991–1992, while Bobby Thigpen of the White Sox set the saves record in 1990 with 57.

Most of these closers had a devastating strikeout pitch, either a blazing fastball, a split-finger sinker, or an unhittable slider. Smith, for example, averaged almost a strikeout an inning during his prime years. In 1989, while pitching for the Boston Red Sox, he struck out 96 batters in 70⅔ innings. Eckersley also was a strikeout pitcher, but what set him apart from most other relievers was his superb control. Between 1989 and 1991 he walked just 16 hitters while pitching 207 innings and striking out 215.

The dominant teams of the 1978–1994 era had outstanding bullpens. The fine Pirate team of the late 1970s depended on the rubber arm of Kent Tekulve and his submarine delivery. Between 1978 and 1980 Tekulve appeared in 263 games, saving 82. In the 1979 World Series an underdog Pirate team defeated the Baltimore Orioles with Tekulve saving three games. The next season the Phillies won their only World Series with reliever Tug McGraw winning one game and saving two others while compiling an ERA of 1.17.

The great Yankee teams of the late 1970s and early 1980s depended on closers such as Sparky Lyle who won a Cy Young award in 1977, winning 13 while saving 26, the fearsome Goose Gossage, whose fastball consistently was clocked in the high 90-miles-per-hour range. Other dominant closers for World

Series winners in this era included Willie Hernandez of the 1984 Tigers, Jesse Orosco of the 1986 Mets, and Eckersley, who anchored the bullpen of the 1989 Oakland A's. None of these teams could have won without its closer.

By the 1980s teams were constructing their pitching staffs around three to four starters and a reliable bullpen. It was a rare manager who left his starters in the game beyond the seventh inning. Earl Weaver, the highly successful skipper of the great Baltimore teams of the 1970s, had a rule of thumb: your starter doesn't pitch in late innings with the game on the line. "That's what you have bullpens for," he argued.

A by-product of this new approach to pitching was the rise in strikeouts in the 1978–1994 era. In these years the batting averages of the American and National leagues did not change dramatically, nor did league ERAs. But the number of strikeouts rose dramatically followed by a sharp rise in home runs.

It had been rare for anyone to strike out 100 times in a season. In 1955, for example, a grand total of three men struck out 100 or more times in both leagues. The number rose slowly but steadily through the 1960s and early 1970s. In 1967 fourteen players exceeded 100 strikeouts. The total began to soar in the late 1970s. The two leagues saw 30 players fan 100 or more times in 1977 as batters began swinging for the fences no matter the cost. Ten years later the figure had risen to 38, and during the 1998 season 73 players fanned 100 or more times.

The American League as a whole recorded 10,150 strikeouts in 1978; the figure rose steadily to more than 13,400 in 1987 and then never dropped below the 12,000 mark.

At the same time there was a steady rise in home runs as more and more players swung for the fences. Gone were the heavy, thick-handled bats that batters once used to put the ball in play. Batters now used light, thin-handled, top-heavy bats that they whipped through the strike zone. If they made contact on the fat part of the bat, the ball would travel great distances.

The National League total of 1,276 homers in 1978 rose to a record 1,824 eight years later. The figures for the American League were similar; 1,680 homers in 1978, 2,634 eight years later. The American League averaged more than 1,980 homers a season during the 1980s while the senior circuit's figure was just under 1,400.

In 1978 in the American League one player hit 40 home runs while four others hit 30. In the National League that same season, one player hit 40 homers while two others hit 30 or more. Eight years later eight National Leaguers hit 30 or more homers while twenty players did so in the American League. Among the American Leaguers topping the 30 mark were eight players who never again hit 30 home runs. Larry Sheets, an unheralded outfielder with the Baltimore Orioles, hit 31 while Mike Pagliarulo of the Yankees dropped from 32 homers to 15 in 1988 and 7 in 1989. Two season later Sheets was a part-timer and hit just 7 homers for the Orioles. Brook Jacoby, a journeyman infielder for Cleveland, hit 34 homers in 1987 and hit 9 the next season. Five years later he was out of baseball.

1987 was a curious season, one of those years when the hitters take charge. Both leagues established the highest batting average and the highest ERA of the 1978–1994 era while setting records for most homers. Leonard Koppett, one of the shrewdest analysts of baseball trends, tested various hypotheses to explain the 1987 offensive explosion. Was the baseball livelier? Could abnormal weather conditions explain this phenomenon? None of his answers satisfied him. While the reasons behind this power surge are not clear, the fans loved this brand of baseball. Attendance for 1987 was 4.5 million above the preceding season, a 9 percent boost and the highest single-season increase since World War II.

Part of baseball's great popularity in the generation after 1978 was due to the quality of the players who predominated during these years. Mike Schmidt, who retired in 1989, is widely recognized as the greatest all-around third baseman in baseball history. In 1995 he was elected to the Hall of Fame. Ozzie Smith, who played into the mid-1990s, redefined defensive play at shortstop and is a certain future Hall of Famer. Tony Gwynn and Wade Boggs, who are still active at this writing, will not only reach the 3,000-hit level but will rank among the best batters in baseball history. As of the end of the 1998 season, Gwynn was tied for seventeenth-place with a .339 average while Boggs was tied with the legendary Honus Wagner for twenty-sixth place with a .329 average. For perspective on their achievements, every player ahead of them is in the Hall of Fame.

George Brett and Robin Yount reached their peak in the 1980s. Both reached 3,000 hits and have been elected to the Hall of Fame. Gary Carter, Johnny Bench, and Carlton Fisk were the best catchers during the decade, team leaders and incredibly durable backstops. Bench is already in the Hall of Fame while Fisk and Carter will eventually wind up there too. Nolan Ryan, Steve Carlton, Phil Niekro, Tom Seaver, and Don Sutton pitched during the 1980s and reached the difficult 300-victory plateau, a feat achieved only twenty times in baseball history. A team of 1978–1994 All Stars would be a match for the best squads in baseball history.

## *Strike Two and Almost Out*

BASEBALL'S GREAT PROSPERITY and its enormous popularity in the 1980s and the early 1990s did not lead to better labor-management relations. In the early 1990s it became increasingly clear that the major league owners were determined to force a showdown with the Players Association and thus regain the control of the sport they had lost in the mid-1970s.

After getting rid of Bowie Kuhn in 1984 they briefly passed power to Peter Ueberroth, who had just successfully managed the 1984 Olympics in Los Angeles. Before he agreed to take the commissioner's job, Ueberroth stipulated that the powers of the office be redefined. The owners turned over to him considerable power to administer the game. Beginning in 1985, at Ueberroth's urging, the owners began to exercise more restraint in bidding for free agents. Sixty-two players filed for free agency after the 1985 season, but not a single one was signed. Marvin Miller immediately cried foul and claimed that the owners were acting in collusion. While it appears that the owners did not collude in a classic sense, Ueberroth had made them consider the economic consequences of their rash bidding for players.

When the Players Association filed a grievance over the absence of offers to free agents in the years 1985–1987, the arbitrator, Thomas Roberts, concluded that the owners had acted to support a common goal, in effect collusion. His finding led to a fine of more than $280 million in damages to compensate the players. The owners were outraged. They got rid of Ueberroth as soon as they could and hired the well-known academic, former president of Yale University, and baseball afficionado Bart Giamatti as new commissioner. Giamatti's powers were less expansive than Ueberroth's, but he had a positive relationship with writers and fans that helped to improve the image of the game. Giamatti genuinely loved baseball; he called it "a public trust."

He was faced almost immediately with a sordid issue— whether Pete Rose, one of baseball's most accomplished and popular players and managers, had bet on baseball games. Giamatti resolved this issue with grace in the summer of 1989 by banishing Rose from baseball. Rose acknowledged that "the commissioner has a factual basis to impose the penalty . . . and agrees not to challenge the penalty in court or otherwise." Unfortunately for baseball, Giamatti died on September 1 of that year after exactly five months as commissioner. His replacement, Fay Vincent, Giamatti's assistant and longtime friend, was named to fill the late commissioner's term, which was to last until 1994. Vincent never made it.

A highly successful corporate lawyer, in the 1980s Vincent had served as president of Columbia Pictures. He knew his way around the corporate boardroom and possessed a shrewd legal mind, but he had never dealt with any group as contentious as the major league owners. He took over as commissioner just as the owners were ready to declare war on the Players Association.

The basic agreement signed in 1990 was just a truce in the war between labor and management. When Vincent began interpreting his powers broadly so as to protect "the good of the game," he was forced out in August 1992. He was replaced by an executive council composed of the presidents of the two major leagues plus eight owners. Milwaukee Brewers president Bud Selig was named chairman, or acting commissioner. In effect the owners would run the game without interference from any commissioner or league president. Major league baseball was preparing for a major attack on the union.

In December 1992 the owners voted to reopen the 1990

basic agreement. Their spokesman, Richard Ravitch, a well-known New York labor negotiator, announced that baseball faced an economic crisis and needed a complete restructuring. He claimed that nineteen teams were losing money. Revenue sharing and a salary cap similar to professional basketball's were necessary to save the National Game.

Sporadic talks between the owners and the Players Association were held throughout the 1993 season, but it was clear that both sides were positioning themselves for a strike. The owners wanted drastic changes in the relationship between labor and management but offered little of value in return. The union was not about to surrender gains won over twenty years. The basic agreement lapsed in December 1993, but talks went on through the 1994 season. Both sides staked out impossible bargaining positions. The owners, for example, suggested that players could apply for free agency after four years instead of six, but with the proviso that the player's club could match any offer. This version of football's Rozelle rule virtually guaranteed that free agency would not work. The Players Association rejected it out of hand, countering with a demand that players be allowed to apply for free agency after just two years. They also wanted the minimum salary increased to $200,000. After an exciting 1993 season which included a new attendance record of 70 million, professional baseball was flourishing. But the labor-management crisis overshadowed the positive aspects of the baseball boom of the 1990s.

The 1994 season started well, featuring three close pennant races—the American and National league had been divided into three divisions each. Players were putting up impressive statistics. Matt Williams of San Francisco was on a pace to challenge Roger Maris's record of 61 home runs while Ken Griffey of Seattle was close behind. Tony Gwynn was batting near the .400 mark all season. Jeff Bagwell, hard-hitting first baseman of the Houston Astros, was driving in more than a run per game and had a slugging percentage of .750, one of the highest since the days of Jimmy Foxx and Babe Ruth. When labor negotiations broke down in August, baseball attendance was on a pace with the 1993 record. If ever there was a year not to have a strike, 1994 was it.

The strike began August 12 and quickly turned ugly. The Players Association issued a report drawn up by Professor Roger Noll of Stanford University that ridiculed the owners' claims of financial hardship as "pure fiction." On the contrary, Noll declared, baseball was "financially healthy."

Acting commissioner Bud Selig announced that unless a resolution of the dispute were reached by September 9, he would cancel the remainder of the season as well as postseason play. All attempts at mediation, including a feeble effort by President Clinton to use the well-known labor mediator William Usery, collapsed. Major league baseball, which had staged a World Series every season since 1905 in spite of two world wars and a Great Depression, wiped out one of the sporting scene's distinguishing features almost without a qualm. It appeared that both sides in the dispute had lost their judgment and common sense. The owners were determined to turn back twenty years of union success while the Players Association refused to admit that baseball had any problems.

Talks continued irregularly throughout the fall and winter of 1994 and early 1995, but the situation grew only more grim. The owners announced that they would play the 1995 season whether the strike was settled or not by using replacement players. This threat to use "scabs" outraged the Players Association, was ridiculed by many sportswriters, and shocked the game's loyal fans.

In March 1995 the National Labor Relations Board filed a preliminary injunction that charged baseball owners with trying to impose a salary cap, end free agency, and engage in collusive activities. U.S. District Judge Sonia Sotomayor of New York granted an injunction on March 31 forestalling these changes, and the union announced that it would end the strike. Selig decided that the season would begin after a slight delay for spring training.

The strike was a catastrophe for baseball. It showed that both sides, owners and players, could not be trusted to protect America's game. The mystique of baseball was shattered as was the fans' trust. If ever there was any doubt about baseball being big business, the 1994 strike ended it. Dave Anderson, sports columnist for the *New York Times,* compared the 1994 strike to the Black Sox scandal of 1919 in the sense of gloom and disenchantment it created among the sport's fans.

Baseball was under a cloud after 1994. When the game returned the next year, fans stayed away in droves. Total attendance of 50 million was down 20 million from 1993's peak. It would be years before baseball recaptured its fans' ardor and enthusiasm.

For three years after the 1994 strike baseball labored unsuccessfully to recapture its hold on the affections of the American public. No baseball player caught the nation's attention as powerfully as did pro basketball's Michael Jordan. The 1995–1997 seasons were failures despite a couple of great teams, especially a revived New York Yankee club led by its popular manager, Joe Torre. Attendance stagnated, and it appeared that baseball had alienated its fan base perhaps permanently. The glow had worn off America's Game. In 1998 major league baseball finally saw its connection to its fans reestablished. It took the great Mark McGwire–Sammy Sosa pursuit of Roger Maris's home run record in 1998 to restore the game's popularity. Fans came out in record numbers to watch these two sluggers shatter all existing home run records—McGwire hit 72, Sosa 66. More than 70.3 million people attended major league games, breaking the record set in 1993, the last year before the strike.

A new basic agreement left the status of baseball basically the same as it was before the 1994 strike. Many of the major questions between the owners and the union remained unresolved. The agreement would come up for renewal in 2000, and there was evidence that some owners wished to force another showdown. If this was true, it was difficult to imagine baseball as we know it surviving.

*The Yale University baseball team, probably 1880.*

## Chapter 10

# THE FUTURE
# OF THE
# NATIONAL GAME

IN ITS VARIOUS GUISES, but especially in its professional form, baseball has been inextricably linked with the course of America's history over the last 175 years. At the beginning of a new millennium, baseball's future is unclear. The game is still recovering from the scars it inflicted on itself in the terrible strike of 1994, and competition from other professional sports, notably football and basketball, are eating away at baseball's fan base. The nation's best athletes no longer choose baseball first. The game is in something of a quiet crisis, a crisis that reflects on management and players alike.

But when wasn't this so? Throughout its rich and colorful history, baseball has somehow managed to survive continuing crises, many of them self-inflicted. The German statesman Bismarck declared, God watches over drunkards, children, and the United States of America. He might have added baseball to his list.

Baseball has survived and often prospered largely because for almost two centuries it has been deeply imbedded in America's roots. More than any other sport, it can truly claim to be uniquely American. With the possible exception of boxing, it is the only sport to spawn a rich and lively body of fiction. Other sports are catching up to baseball in many ways, but they have yet to produce their own literature.

Baseball touches a nerve deep in America's psyche, perhaps something as elemental as the nation's longing for a lost age of innocence. The popularity in recent years of films such as *Field of Dreams* and *Angels in the Outfield* testifies to America's belief that there once was a purer time in baseball's history. Of course, this is a myth. Baseball was never played in a Garden of Eden. At least from the time of the game's professionalization in the late 1860s and early 1870s, baseball has been a fiercely competitive business which attracts players and owners for its promise of money, fame, and popular adulation.

Yet baseball has always been more than a mere search for wealth. The country grew up playing baseball, and for a long time the sport had no serious rival for fans' interest. The game evolved and grew just as the country was transformed from a rural to an urban society. Baseball began in the cities of the Northeast in the 1830s and 1840s, but within a single generation it spread to the rural Midwest where it was eagerly adopted as a sign of modernization.

Knowledge and understanding of the game has been passed from one generation to the next. Part of its appeal can be traced to the fact that since the introduction of overhand pitching and the fixing of the distance between the pitcher and home plate at 60 feet, 6 inches, baseball essentially has not changed. A person watching a game today is sharing an experience that is little different from what it was more than a century ago. That is not the case with other modern sports in America, which bear little resemblance to their beginnings.

As America became increasingly urban, baseball took root in the expanding cities. It is interesting to note that the date usually given for the emergence of modern professional baseball, Ban Johnson's founding of the American League in 1901 came at a time when Americans in large numbers were moving from rural to urban areas. The growth of modern baseball thus paralleled the growing urbanization of the nation in the twentieth century.

Baseball's growth in the cities also sheds light on another source of its appeal. It began essentially as an upper-middle- to middle-class White Anglo-Saxon Protestant attempt to create a club sport for America similar to cricket in England. But as early as the 1870s the game began to integrate outsiders. The first of the immigrant groups to embrace baseball were German Americans, followed shortly by Irish Americans. Both used baseball as a way of gaining acceptance in a society that viewed them as outsiders—the Germans because of their language and culture, the Irish because of their religion and other curious customs such as drinking and brawling. By the 1890s these former outsiders had matched the older established groups in their impact on baseball.

The experience of the Irish illustrated a trend that would continue throughout baseball's modern history: an ethnic or racial group, through its skills and talents, gains admission to the game, wins acceptance, and in the process helps undermine the prejudice against it.

In the 1880s the Irish produced baseball's first superstar or celebrity (in the modern sense of the term), Mike "King" Kelly. Like his contemporary Irishman, heavyweight champion John L. Sullivan, Kelly could easily be stereotyped. Both men were hard-drinking, crude, loud, flashy individuals who conformed to society's view of the immigrant Irish. While this stereotype would persist for another generation, other Irish baseball players would redefine America's Game. The concept of the modern manager can be traced to two Irish Americans, John McGraw and Connie Mack.

McGraw favored a style of inside baseball—always looking for the edge, taunting his adversary into mistakes—that was adopted by managers such as Leo Durocher, Gene Mauch, Casey Stengel, and Frankie Frisch. Mack was the more cerebral manager, stressing good pitching, playing the game the way a gentleman would. His successors would include some of baseball's best skippers—Joe McCarthy, Sparky Anderson, Walter Alston.

German Americans produced some of baseball's greatest players—Lou Gehrig, Babe Ruth, Honus Wagner. While they did not have to overcome the degree of prejudice directed at Irish Americans, the ethnic slur of "squarehead" or "dumb Dutchman" plagued them too.

These two groups were the forerunners of other ethnics who would use baseball with varying degrees of success to gain acceptance. Poles, Italians, and Jews made their breakthrough in the late 1920s and early 1930s. Al Simmons, Joe DiMaggio, and Hank Greenberg became national heroes whose popularity transcended their ethnic group. In the 1930s, when American isolationism thrived, two of the most popular baseball players were thus a Jew and an Italian, who with the black heavyweight champ Joe Louis helped undermine the terrible ethnic and racial prejudice of the recent past.

After World War II, when racial bars came down, the blacks—with greater difficulty—were able to duplicate the success of other ethnic groups and use baseball as a route to success. Since the time of Jackie Robinson, black players have been among the most popular in major league baseball. Willie Mays is often regarded as the greatest player of his generation (1950–1970). He was followed by other equally successful black players—Bob Gibson, Reggie Jackson, Joe Morgan, and today one of the most highly regarded players in baseball, Ken Griffey, Jr.

The struggles of black players to win acceptance were greater than those experienced by their Irish, German, Jewish, or Italian counterparts because of the depth of racial prejudice in America. But by the 1960s black players had proven themselves, and their proportional representation in the major leagues was greater than in American society. Within a few years the first black manager and general manager emerged. Today, while the problems of blacks at the managerial level persist, the trend in professional baseball is clearly positive.

Latin players, when they appeared in large numbers in the late 1950s and early 1960s, found a different yet nonetheless difficult path to acceptance. Many Latin players were not only foreign but also black, thus they experienced a double prejudice. They also were treated in stereotypical fashion as the happy-go-lucky, always smiling, flashy hot dog. While the language problem persists and Latin players have not made the same progress at the managerial level as American blacks, their sheer numbers are transforming baseball today. Over the past two decades the greatest pool of baseball talent has been Latin American. Unlike in the United States, there is no other sport in Latin America, with the possible exception of soccer, to rival baseball for the affections of the people. The best Latin American athletes continue to choose baseball. The most successful major league teams have mined Latin America the way Branch Rickey did the Negro Leagues. In Sammy Sosa, the great home run hitter of the Chicago Cubs, Latin America has produced its first national celebrity, bigger than Roberto Clemente of the Pirates or Juan Marichal of the Giants ever was. By carrying himself with such charm and dignity during the assault on Roger Maris's home run record in 1998, Sosa endeared himself to baseball fans and to the American public at large.

In the *Baseball Register* for 1999, which lists every player on major league rosters, the most common name today is not Jones, Smith, or Williams; it is Martinez. This trend will continue. American baseball in the future will have a Latin accent.

The next wave of baseball talent will undoubtedly be Asian. Already Hideo Nomo and Hideki Irabu have shown the potential of Asian players. Unlike the Latins, however, Asian players can turn to a highly successful league of their own, in Japan. It is not yet clear that major league baseball will be as successful in recruiting talent from Asia as it has from Latin America.

Baseball's diversity in an age of growing emphasis on multiculturalism has a better record than any other professional sport in America. Latins or Asians are rare in football or basketball. Baseball remains what it has been for a century: an avenue for oppressed ethnic or racial groups to win acceptance by the quality of their play in America's Game.

For better or worse, baseball's future is tied to television. Television brings enormous revenues to the sport and increasingly forces the game to accommodate itself to the media. Initial fears that television would keep fans at home have faded. Despite cable and the rise of superstations, game attendance has increased to record levels. Even with the terrible strike of 1994, the 1990s will easily top attendance figures for any past decade.

Baseball has in fact adjusted beautifully to television. When the game was first telecast on the small screen, camera work was poor and it was difficult for the viewer to follow a small white ball against a black and white background. Today such problems have been overcome. Color, the use of many cameras at different levels, and especially slow-motion replays have highlighted the skills and athleticism of today's ball players.

The chief problem that television presents to baseball today is an imbalance in revenues. For the foreseeable future certain teams will command enormous TV revenues while so-called small-market teams such as Pittsburgh or the Minnesota Twins will have limited income from television. Combined with teams that have superstations, such as Atlanta, Chicago, and New York, this skewed revenue could lead to the permanent dominance of a small group of teams. The most successful teams in the 1990s have been wealthy ones such as Atlanta and the Yankees, both with lucrative television contracts.

Unless baseball finds some way to share television revenues as professional football does, it is difficult to see how small-market teams will be able to compete.

Finally, players and management continue to wrestle with the sharing of profits that have accrued in recent years. Baseball's great prosperity spawned two work stoppages, in 1981 and 1994, that in the final analysis really concerned who would control the game. The owners, the Lords of Baseball, have run the sport since its infancy but have lost power to a well-focused, well-led players association. This issue has not been resolved, though fan reaction to the 1994 strike sent a shiver through both camps. Another showdown may occur early in the new century. If so, given the challenge from other professional sports, baseball's future could once again be in jeopardy.

# Notes

## Chapter 1: Origins of the Game

page 5, line 21: on baseball changing more than cricket, see Steven Gelber, "Their Hands Are All Out Playing: Business and Amateur Baseball, 1845–1917," *Journal of Sport History*, XI, no. 1 (Spring 1984), p. 7.

page 6, line 17: on the class background of early players, see Melvin Adelman, *A Sporting Time: New York City and the Rise of Modern Athletics, 1820–70* (Urbana, Ill., 1986), pp. 123–182.

page 9, line 18: on the significance of Chadwick's innovations, see David Lamoreaux, "Baseball in the Nineteenth Century: The Source of Its Appeal," *Journal of Popular Culture*, II, no. 3 (1977), p. 599.

page 13, line 9: George B. Kirsch, "Bats, Balls and Bullets: Baseball and the Civil War," *Civil War Times*, May 1998, pp. 30–37.

page 13, line 15: information on college baseball is from Ronald Smith, "The Rise of College Baseball," *Baseball History*, I (1986), pp. 23–41.

page 13, line 26: details of nineteenth-century baseball are from the special issue edited by John Thorn and Mark Rucker, "The Nineteenth Century," *The National Pastime*, Spring 1984.

page 17, line 3: details of the Reds' loss are from George Bulkley, "The Day the Reds Lost," *The National Pastime*, Fall 1982, p. 7.

page 22, line 18: on Spalding's tour of Britain, see Neil Stout, "1874 Baseball: Not Cricket to the British," *Baseball Research Journal*, 1985, pp. 83–85.

## Chapter 2: Baseball as Big Business, 1876–1891

page 26, line 4: the Twain quote may be found in Lewis Carlson, "The Universal Athletic Sport of the World," *American History Illustrated*, April 1984, p. 37.

page 31, line 28: the significance of the National Agreement is developed in Harold Seymour, *Baseball: The Early Years* (New York, 1960), pp. 145–147.

page 32, line 8: on the role of Arthur Soden and the reserve clause, see Frederick Ivor-Campbell, "Arthur Soden," *Baseball's First Stars* (Cleveland, 1996), p. 153.

page 32, line 27: on Kelly's income, see Seymour, *Early Years*, p. 117.

page 35, line 32: Anson's refusal to play against black players is from Jerry Malloy, "Out at Home: Baseball Draws the Color Line," *The National Pastime*, Spring 1985, p. 25.

page 35, line 12: Jerry Malloy, ed., *Sol White's History of Colored Base Ball* (Lincoln, Nebr., 1995), p. xxiv.

page 36, line 29: on baseball's drinking men, see Bill James, *The Bill James Historical Baseball Abstract* (New York, 1988), p. 26.

page 39, line 29: on "Casey at the Bat," see Tristan P. Coffin, *The Old Ball Game* (New York, 1971), p. 160; on the possibility that Kelly was the model for Casey, see Charles O'Brien Kennedy, ed., *American Ballads: Naughty, Ribald and Classic* (New York, 1952), p. 132.

page 41, line 7: on A. J. Reach, see Charles Middleton, "Alfred 'Al' Reach," in David Porter, ed., *Biographical Dictionary of American Sports: Baseball*, I (New York, 1987), 464–465.

page 41, line 27: on the Baker Bowl see Rich Westcott, *Philadelphia's Old Ballparks* (Philadelphia, 1996), p. 29.

page 42, line 18: on the figure won by St. Louis, see James, *Baseball Abstract*, p. 31.

page 42, line 23: on the point about the players dividing the money equally, see Robert Smith, *Illustrated History of Baseball* (New York, 1973), p. 66.

page 43, line 3: the figures on American Association attendance are from David Voigt, "Out with the Crowds: Counting, Courting and Controlling Baseball Ballpark Fans," *Baseball History*, II (1989), 94.

page 43, line 27: the application of the concept of status deprivation as applied to baseball players is from David Voigt, *American Baseball* (University Park, Pa., 1970), I, 190.

page 44, line 33: Spalding's profit for the world tour is from Peter Levine, "Business, Missionary Motives Behind the 1888–1889 World Tour," *Baseball Research Journal,* XIII (1984), p. 61.

## Chapter 3: Coming of Age, 1891–1908

page 53, line 21: attendance figures for the 1890s are from James, *Baseball Abstract,* p. 43.

page 53, line 26: on the result of the split-season format, see Voigt, *American Baseball,* I, 247.

page 55, line 1: on the division of revenues in the championship series, see Seymour, *Early Years,* pp. 288–289.

page 55, line 18: information on the playoff system in the 1890s is from Jerry Lansche, *The Forgotten Championships: PostSeason Baseball, 1882–1981* (Jefferson, N.C., 1989).

page 56, line 11: the Heydler quote is from Seymour, *Early Years,* p. 290.

page 57, line 17: *Ibid.,* p. 269.

page 58, line 4: for the viciousness of early basketball, see Benjamin Rader, *American Sports: From the Age of Folk Games to the Age of Televised Sports,* 2nd ed. (Englewood Cliffs, N.J., 1990), p. 218.

page 59, line 19: the players' hatred of Freeman is from Seymour, *Early Years,* p. 297.

page 61, line 32: for Johnson's conviction that the American League would overtake the National, see Geoffrey Ward, *Baseball: An Illustrated History* (New York, 1994), p. 65.

page 63, line 13: Collins's quote is from Joseph Overfield, "James Joseph Collins," *Baseball's First Stars* (Cleveland, 1996), p. 39.

page 65, line 21: the quote about the two leagues coexisting is from *The National League of Professional Baseball Clubs vs. the Federal Club of Baltimore,* Washington D.C. Court of Appeals, 1920, pp. 681–684.

page 69, line 4: for Brush and McGraw's reasons for not playing a World Series in 1904, see Ward, *Baseball,* p. 69.

page 70, line 9: the rumors about Waddell are from Seymour, *Baseball: The Golden Years* (New York, 1960), p. 15.

page 71, line 21: on college players in baseball, see Steven Riess, "Race and Ethnicity in American Baseball, 1900–1919," *Journal of Ethnic Studies,* IV, no. 4 (1977), pp. 44–45.

## Chapter 4: The Wars of Baseball, 1909–1918

page 76, line 12: the material on Shibe Park is found in Bruce Kuklick, *To Every Thing a Season: Shibe Park and Urban Philadelphia, 1909–1976* (Princeton, 1991), p. 28

page 77, line 29: for the cost of building Shibe Park, see *ibid.*, p. 25.

page 78, line 24: on attendance at games in Pittsburgh, see Lowell Reidenbaugh, *Take Me Out to the Ball Park* (St. Louis, 1986), p. 221.

page 80, line 12: the quote on Cobb having to be first comes from David Phillips and Lawrence Kart, *That Old Ball Game* (Chicago, 1975), p. 55.

page 83, line 11: on baseball's competition from the movies, see James, *Baseball Abstract,* p. 101.

page 84, line 10: on baseball's gross income in the second decade of the century, see Voigt, *American Baseball,* II, 108–109.

page 85, line 20: Gary Hailey, "Anatomy of a Murder: The Federal League and the Courts," *The National Pastime,* Spring 1985, p. 63.

page 88, line 15: for the figure for the sale of the A's players, see Seymour, *Golden Years,* p. 220

page 88, line 24: on the losses of the Federal League, see Steven Riess, *Sport in Industrial America, 1850–1920* (Wheeling, Ill., 1995), p. 176.

page 89, line 4: Gilmore's conviction that the Federal League was doomed is from Hailey, "Anatomy of a Murder," p. 66.

page 90, line 24: the quote about Baltimore being a minor league town is from *ibid.*, p. 70.

## Chapter 5: Golden Age, 1919–1931

page 99, line 31: for Johnson's troubles in the American League, see Seymour, *Golden Years,* p. 268.

page 103, line 2: the best summary of the Black Sox scandal remains Eliot Asinof, *Eight Men Out* (Chicago, 1963).

page 105, line 11: for information on Ruth, see Marshall Smelser, *The Life That Ruth Built* (Lincoln, Nebr., 1975).

page 106, line 26: possible candidates for commissioner of baseball is from Clark Nardinelli, "Judge Kenesaw Mountain Landis and the Art of Cartel Enforcement," *Baseball History,* I (1989), p. 103.

page 107, line 9: the quote on supporting Landis can be found in Norman Rosenberg, "Here Comes the Judge: The Origins of Baseball's Commissioner System and American Legal Culture," *Journal of Popular Culture*, XX, no. 4 (Spring 1987), p. 135.

page 107, line 12: baseball being fortunate in naming Landis is from Seymour, *Golden Age*, II, 320.

page 112, line 15: material on Foster and the Negro League can be found in Ward, *Baseball*, as well as in Bruce Chadwick, *When the Game Was Black and White: An Illustrated History of the Negro Leagues* (New York, 1992) and Robert Patterson, *Only the Ball Was White: A History of the Legendary Black Players and All-Black Professional Teams* (New York, 1989).

page 113, line 15: statistical material on ERA is from Benjamin Rader, *Baseball: A History of America's Game* (Urbana, Ill., 1992), p. 115.

page 114, line 21: for information on Lou Gehrig, see Ray Robinson, *Iron Horse: Lou Gehrig in His Time* (New York, 1990).

page 116, line 4: for Rickey's concept of the farm system, Murray Polner, *Branch Rickey: A Biography* (New York, 1982).

page 118, line 5: the financial figures come from Bill Rabinowitz, "Baseball and the Great Depression," *Baseball History*, I (1989), p. 14.

## Chapter 6: Baseball in Depression and War, 1931–1945

page 123, line 6: Rader, *Baseball*, p. 50.

page 124, line 4: Frank Bilovsky and Rich Westcott, *The Phillies Encyclopedia* (Philadelphia, 1993), p. 473.

page 124, line 18: for Mack's sale of his players in the mid-1930s, see Kuklick, *To Every Thing a Season*, p. 63.

page 127, line 23: on MacPhail, see Don Warfield, *The Roaring Redhead: Larry MacPhail, Baseball's Great Innovator* (South Bend, Ind., 1987).

page 128, line 26: the McCarthy quote can be found in Harvey Frommer, *Baseball's Greatest Managers* (New York, 1985), p. 154.

page 130, line 19: for a good picture of how the Yankees worked, see Tommy Henrich with Bill Gilbert, *Five O'Clock Lightning* (New York, 1992).

page 136, line 8: for a good overview of baseball changes in the 1930s, see G. Edward White, *Creating the National Pastime: Baseball Transforms Itself, 1903–1953* (Princeton, 1996), pp. 119–125, as well as Chapter 5 on night baseball and Chapter 7, which deals with baseball's adoption of radio broadcasting.

page 138, line 9: for the Hall of Fame, the best source is Bill James, *The Politics of Glory: How Baseball's Hall of Fame Really Works* (New York, 1994).

page 138, line 17: baseball's fear of radio is in White, *Creating the National Pastime*, p. 240.

page 139, line 5: for the Gillette deal, see Benjamin Rader, *In Its Own Image: How Television Transformed Sports* (New York, 1984), p. 25.

page 140, line 14: the *Sporting News* quote is from Rabinowitz, "Baseball and the Great Depression," p. 55; White, *Creating the National Pastime*, pp. 168–169.

page 140, line 22: on night baseball being a novelty, see Mark Ribowsky, *The Power and the Darkness* (New York, 1996), pp. 45–46.

page 142, line 10: a good study of Roosevelt's green light for baseball during World War II is James A. Percoco, "Baseball and World War II: A Study of the Landis-Roosevelt Correspondence," *Magazine of History*, VII, no. 1, pp. 55–60.

page 142, line 28: the analysis of who played war time baseball is from Harrington Crissey, *Teenagers, Graybeards, and 4-Fs: An Informal History of Major League Baseball During the Second World War* (Privately printed, 1982).

page 144, line 6: for an overview of World War II baseball, see Bill Gilbert, *They Also Served: Baseball and the Home Front, 1941–1945* (New York, 1992) and William Mead, *Even the Browns* (Chicago, 1978).

## Chapter 7: No Golden Age: Baseball, 1946–1960

page 148, line 6: the *Fortune* quote is from Landon Y. Jones, *Great Expectations* (New York, 1980), p. 20.

page 151, line 12: the offer to Newhouser can be found in David Jordan, *A Tiger in His Time: Hal Newhouser and the Burden of Wartime Ball* (South Bend, Ind., 1990), p. 174.

page 151, line 30: the Marion quote is from the *New York Times,* September 8, 1946, p. 29.

page 153, line 6: on the threat to use Wagner, see John P. Rossi, *A Whole New Game: Off the Field Changes in Baseball, 1946–1960* (Jefferson, N.C., 1999), p. 11.

page 153, line 22: the instruction of the pension program in 1946 is covered in Frederick Turner, *When the Boys Came Back: Baseball and 1946* (New York, 1996), p. 197.

page 154, line 7: for an overview of the years 1946–1960, see Rossi, *A Whole New Game.*

page 154, line 23: for Rickey's signing of talent during the war, see Ed Linn with Leo Durocher, *Nice Guys Finish Last* (New York, 1975), p. 219.

page 155, line 21: the Feller quote is from Peter Golenbock, *Bums—An Oral History of the Brooklyn Dodgers* (New York, 1984), p. 144.

page 156, line 4: Robinson's significance is traced in Jules Tygiel, *Baseball's Great Experiment: Jackie Robinson and His Legacy* (New York, 1997) and Robinson's own autobiography, *I Never Had It Made: An Autobiography* as told to Alfred Duckett (Hopewell, N.J., 1995).

page 159, line 5: the figures on the impact of television are from Rader, *American Sports,* p. 255.

page 161, line 26: the best study of the move to Baltimore is James Miller, *The Baseball Business: Pursuing Pennants and Profits in Baltimore* (Chapel Hill, 1990).

page 164, line 13: the Stoneham quote can be found in Neil Sullivan, *The Dodgers Move West* (New York, 1987), p. 133.

## Chapter 8: Coming Apart, 1961–1977

page 174, line 12: on the popularity of football, see Rader, *American Sports,* pp. 268–269.

page 176, line 27: for baseball's problems in the late 1960s, see Ron Briley, "It Was 20 Years Ago Today: Baseball Responds to the Unrest of 1968," *Baseball History,* I (1989), pp. 82–91.

page 180, line 14: for attendance discrepancies between the two leagues, see James, *Baseball Abstract,* p. 160.

page 181, line 32: on CBS's purchase of the Yankees, see the *Sporting News Baseball Guide, 1965,* p. 154.

page 186, line 22: for Miller, see his autobiography, *A Whole Different Ball Game: The Sport and Business of Baseball* (New York, 1991).

page 186, line 28: the Veeck quote is from the *Sporting News Baseball Guide, 1973,* p. 269.

page 188, line 20: the Seitz quote is from *ibid., 1976,* p. 288.

## Chapter 9: Best of Times, Worst of Times, 1978–1994

page 194, line 29: the Peters quote is from the *Sporting News Baseball Guide, 1982* pp. 12–13.

page 197, line 2: James Quirk and Rodney D. Fort, *Pay Dirt: The Business of Professional Team Sports* (Princeton, 1992), pp. 507–508.

page 197, line 16: *ibid.*, p. 122.

page 201, line 33, for the various explanations for the increase in hitting, Leonard Koppett, *The New Thinking Fan's Guide to Baseball* (New York, 1991), pp. 348–349.

page 202, line 4: on the attendance increase in 1987, see James, *Baseball Abstract*, p. 267.

page 206, line 12: the Noll quote is from the *Sporting News Baseball Guide, 1995*, p. 180.

page 207, line 16: Anderson's quote is from Street and Smith's *Baseball Yearbook*, 1995, p. 6.

# A Note on Sources

HEMINGWAY SAID that all modern American fiction began with Huckleberry Finn. The serious study of baseball also started with one book, Harold Seymour's groundbreaking two-volume attempt to wed scholarly research and baseball history, *Baseball: The Early Years* and *The Golden Years* (New York, 1960). Seymour opened a new field of study by showing that one could link the evolution of baseball with major themes of American history. I have relied heavily on his analysis of early nineteenth-century baseball, the so-called lost years of baseball history. A third Seymour volume, *The People's Game* (New York, 1989), reaches beyond the professional game of baseball to analyze the sport's hold on the public's mind.

Next to Seymour in significance for the serious study of baseball history is the work of David Voigt. His three-volume *American Baseball* (University Park, Pa., 1983) continues what Seymour started but carries the story of the professional game to the near-present. I also found his short study, *America Through Baseball* (Chicago, 1976), suggestive of new approaches to the study of baseball's links to the nation's past. Voigt's work stresses the role of baseball in the development of a leisure revolution in America in the late nineteenth and early twentieth centuries.

An idiosyncratic but highly effective way of conceptualizing developments in baseball from its origins to the present can be found in Bill James, *The Bill James Historical Baseball Abstract*

(New York, 1988). James breaks the game down decade by decade while isolating key themes that transformed the sport. His book contains sections on "drinking men," the evolution of baseball uniforms, and a listing of the best baseball books by decade. Equally interesting for an analysis of baseball over the years is a book by a former sportswriter who has challenged encrusted thinking about the game: Leonard Koppett's *The New Thinking Fan's Guide to Baseball* (New York, 1991) is a key work for understanding the internal complexities of the game.

One can find a valuable overview of baseball history in its broadest context in Jonathan Fraser Light, *The Cultural Encyclopedia of Baseball* (Jefferson, N.C., 1997), a gold mine of esoteric information.

A number of general histories provide valuable insights on the evolution of baseball in American life. Among the best are Robert Smith, *An Illustrated History of Baseball* (New York, 1973); David Voigt, *Baseball: An Illustrated History* (University Park, Pa., 1983); and Geoffrey Ward, *Baseball: An Illustrated History* (New York, 1994). Ward's book grew out of Ken Burns's enormously successful public television series on baseball. It has a superb collection of evocative photographs illustrating the various dimensions of the game.

At a different level are certain scholarly histories of American sports. Two of the most useful are by Benjamin Rader. His *American Sports: From the Age of Folk Games to the Age of Televised Sports* (Englewood Cliffs, N.J., 1990) places baseball in the context of the development of sport in American history. *Baseball: A History of America's Game* (Urbana, Ill., 1992) is a succinct overview which concentrates on professional baseball. Charles Alexander, *Our Game: An American Baseball History* (New York, 1991) is splendidly written and incorporates the latest research on baseball's past.

Much original research in recent years has been directed at unearthing new information about baseball's early development. Among the best of these studies is Melvin Adelman, *A Sporting Time: New York City and the Rise of Modern Athletics, 1820–70*

(Urbana, Ill, 1986). On the class makeup of nineteenth-century fans, Allen Guttmann's *Sports Spectators* (New York, 1986) argues that they came largely from the lower classes. Adelman, on the other hand, believes the evidence indicates that most fans in baseball's early years were middle class. See his "Spectators and Crowds in Sport History: A Critical Analysis of Allen Guttmann's 'Sports Spectators,' " *Journal of Sport History*, XIV (1987).

Some of the best work on early baseball has appeared in essay form. Steven Gelber, "Their Hands Are All Out Playing: Business and Amateur Baseball, 1845–1917," *Journal of Sport History*, XI, no. 1 (1984); David Lamoreaux, "Baseball in the Nineteenth Century: The Source of Its Appeal," *Journal of Popular Culture*, II, no. 3 (1977); and Lewis Carlson, "The Universal Athletic Sport of the World," *American History Illustrated*, April 1984, are useful for explaining baseball's growing appeal in the nineteenth century. At a different level I found Marshall Wright, *Nineteenth-Century Baseball: Year-by-Year Statistics for the Major League Teams, 1871 through 1900* (Jefferson, N.C., 1996) useful for checking detailed statistical information.

The growing sophistication of baseball in the last quarter of the nineteenth century is emphasized in Peter Levine, *A. G. Spalding and the Rise of Baseball* (New York, 1985). Spalding was one of the key figures in transforming baseball into a major business. He also stressed the role of patriotism in spreading baseball's popularity in the United States. He was a major proponent of the idea that baseball was a unique American invention, one that owed nothing to any other nation.

A good source of information on nineteenth-century players and executives is a publication of the Society of American Baseball Research (SABR): Frederick Ivor-Campbell, Robert L. Tiemann, and Mark Rucker, eds., *Baseball's First Stars* (Cleveland, 1996). The product of many scholars and baseball aficionados, it contains brief sketches of key figures in the game's early development.

For baseball's development in the first quarter of the twentieth century, one can supplement Seymour and Voigt with some excellent new biographies that have appeared in recent years. I found particularly useful Charles Alexander, *John McGraw* (New York, 1988); Arthur D. Hittner, *Honus Wagner: The Life of Baseball's "Flying Dutchman,"* (Jefferson, N.C., 1996); and Charles Alexander, *Ty Cobb* (New York, 1988). Also valuable for this period is Lawrence Ritter, *The Glory of Their Times: The Story of the Early Days of Baseball Told by the Men Who Played It* (New York, 1984). Ritter broke new ground with his techniques of weaving interviews together with historical analysis. Others followed his lead most effectively: Donald Honig, *Baseball in the '30s: A Decade of Survival* (New York, 1989) and *Baseball in the '50s: A Decade of Transition* (New York, 1987).

The construction of new ballparks in the second decade of the twentieth century is treated in Michael Gershman, *Diamonds: The Evolution of the Ballpark* (Boston, 1992); Lowell Reidenbaugh, *Take Me Out to the Ball Park* (St. Louis, 1983); Lawrence Ritter, *Lost Ballparks: A Celebration of Baseball's Legendary Fields* (New York, 1992); and Rich Westcott, *Philadelphia's Old Ballparks* (Philadelphia, 1996). A different approach is Bruce Kuklick's *To Every Thing a Season: Shibe Park and Urban Philadelphia 1909–1976* (Princeton, 1991). Kuklick traces the connections over the years between Shibe Park and the community that grew up around it. His book combines baseball with social history.

A scholarly approach to baseball in the early twentieth century is the work of Steven Riess in *Sport in Industrial America, 1850–1920* (Wheeling, Ill., 1995), *City Games: The Evolution of American Urban Society and the Rise of Sports* (Urbana, Ill., 1991), and *Touching Base: Professional Baseball and American Culture in the Progressive Era* (Westport, Conn., 1980). His short essay "Race and Ethnicity in American Baseball, 1900–1919," *Journal of Ethnic Studies*, IV, no. 4 (1977), shows baseball attracting a surprisingly large number of college men in the early years of the century. He also rejects the idea that the sport was a source of upward mobility at this time.

The Federal League challenge to major league baseball is treated in detail by Seymour and Voigt. Their work can be supplemented by Joseph M. Wayman, "Federal League Legacies," *Base-*

*ball Research Journal*, no. 26 (1997) and Gary Hailey, "Anatomy of a Murder: The Federal League and the Courts," *The National Pastime*, 1986. Hailey's article analyzes the legal challenge brought by Baltimore against the major leagues on anti-trust grounds that eventually reached the Supreme Court.

The Supreme Court decision granting baseball special protection from the Sherman Anti-Trust and Clayton Acts is treated in detail by Seymour, *Golden Years*, pp. 211–232. It can be supplemented by Joseph J. McMahon, Jr., and John P. Rossi, "A History and Analysis of Baseball's Three Antitrust Exemptions," *Villanova Sports and Entertainment Law Forum*, II (1995). The case itself is *Federal Baseball Club, Inc., v. National League of Professional Baseball Clubs*, Supreme Court, 1922.

For the Black Sox scandal, Eliot Asinof, *Eight Men Out* (Chicago, 1963) is still the best single study. Dean Smith, "The Black Sox Scandal," *American History Illustrated*, January 1977; Norman Rosenberg, "Here Comes the Judge: The Origins of Baseball's Commissioner System and American Legal Culture," *Journal of Popular Culture*, XX, no. 4 (1987); and Kent M. Krause, "Regulating the Baseball Cartel: A Reassessment of the National Commission, Judge Landis and the Anti-Trust Exemption," *International Journal of the History of Sport*, XIV, no. 1 (1997) all take a slightly different approach from Asinof's.

For an overview of developments in baseball between the emergence of the power game in 1920 to the end of World War II, G. Edward White, *Creating the National Pastime: Baseball Transforms Itself, 1903–1953* (Princeton, 1996) and Richard Crepeau, *Baseball, America's Diamond Mind, 1919–1941* (Orlando, Fla., 1980) are useful. Eugene Murdock, *Baseball Between the Wars: Memories of the Game by the Men Who Played It* (Westport, Conn., 1992) uses interviews to tell the story of baseball in the 1920s and the depression years. White's book is particularly good on developments in the 1930s as baseball struggled to adopt new approaches such as the radio broadcasting of games and night baseball. The best study of the individual most responsible for these innovations can be found in Don Warfield, *The Roaring*

*Redhead: Larry MacPhail, Baseball's Great Innovator* (South Bend, Ind., 1987). Crepeau also wrote a clever essay, "Pearl Harbor: A Failure of Baseball," *Journal of Popular Culture*, XVI (September 1982), which shows that many Americans believed that sport, in this case baseball, could serve to create good feelings between potential enemies.

For the story of the development of the Hall of Fame, a good starting point is Bill James, *The Politics of Glory: How Baseball's Hall of Fame Really Works* (New York, 1994). G. Edward White also has interesting material on the baseball establishment's approach to the idea of a Hall of Fame.

There are many fine biographies of key players from the 1920–1945 era. Marshall Smelser, *The Life That Ruth Built* (New York, 1975) and Robert Creamer, *Babe: The Legend Comes to Life* (New York, 1974) effectively analyze the life and times of baseball's greatest player, Babe Ruth. Ray Robinson, *Iron Horse: Lou Gehrig in His Time* (New York, 1990) provides insight into the development of the great Yankee dynasty of the 1920s and 1930s. Charles Alexander, *Rogers Hornsby: A Biography* (New York, 1995) is a beautifully written life of this talented but difficult ballplayer and manager. William C. Kashatus, *Connie Mack's '29 Triumph: The Rise and Fall of the Philadelphia Athletics Dynasty* (Jefferson, N.C., 1999) tells the story of the great A's team of the late 1920s and early 1930s. Robert Hood, *The Gashouse Gang* (New York, 1976) uses interviews to tell the story of one of the most successful teams in National League history.

The literature on the development of the Negro leagues has grown in recent years. Robert Peterson, *Only the Ball Was White* (Englewood Cliffs, N.J., 1970); John Holway, *Black Diamonds: Life in the Negro Leagues from the Men Who Lived It* (Westport, Conn., 1989); and Bruce Chadwick, *When the Game Was Black and White: An Illustrated History of the Negro Leagues* (New York, 1992) are solidly written overviews of black baseball. Ward, *Baseball,* has an excellent chapter on Rube Foster.

For baseball during World War II there are a number of good sources. Robert Creamer, *Baseball in '41: A Celebration of the Best*

*Baseball Season Ever—in the Year America Went to War* (New York, 1992) examines the dramatic season that saw Joe DiMaggio hit in fifty-six consecutive games and Ted Williams became the last major leaguer to hit .400. Harrington E. Crissey, *Teenagers, Gray-beards, and 4-Fs,* 2 vols. (Privately published, 1982); William Mead, *Even the Browns* (Chicago, 1978); and Bill Gilbert, *They Also Served: Baseball and the Home Front, 1941–1945* (New York, 1992) cover the topic well.

The immediate postwar era has attracted attention in recent years. William Marshall, *Baseball's Pivotal Era, 1945–1951* (Lexington, Ky., 1999) sees baseball playing a significant role in the changes sweeping over America in the immediate aftermath of the war. John P. Rossi, *A Whole New Game: Off the Field Changes in Baseball, 1946–1960* (Jefferson, N.C., 1999) argues that for all its problems, baseball creatively dealt with challenges such as integration, franchise shifts, and the emergence of television. Frederick Turner, *When the Boys Came Back: Baseball and 1946* (New York, 1996) and Roger Kahn, *The Era, 1947–1957, When the Yankees, the Giants, and the Dodgers Ruled the World* (New York, 1993) are good general overviews.

The story of the integration of baseball can be followed in two studies of baseball's "Mahatma," Branch Rickey: Murray Polner, *Branch Rickey: A Biography* (New York, 1982) and Arthur Mann, *Branch Rickey: American in Action* (Boston, 1957). The best study of Jackie Robinson's travail remains Jules Tygiel, *Baseball's Great Experiment: Jackie Robinson and His Legacy* (New York, 1983). It can be supplemented with Robinson's autobiography, *I Never Had It Made: An Autobiography* as told to Alfred Duckett (Hopewell, N.J., 1995).

There are a number of good biographies and memoirs for the years after World War II. Ed Linn with Leo Durocher, *Nice Guys Finish Last* (New York, 1975); Lou Boudreau with Russell Schneider, *Lou Boudreau: Covering All the Bases* (Champaign, Ill., 1993); Harold Parrott, *The Lords of Baseball* (New York, 1976); and Red Barber, *1947: When All Hell Broke Loose in Baseball* (Garden City, N.Y., 1982) are among the best. Parrott, who was traveling secretary for the Brooklyn Dodgers for twenty years, paints wonderful portraits of Rickey and Durocher.

In a class by itself is David Halberstam, *The Summer of '49* (New York, 1989). Halberstam uses his considerable skills to tell the story of the rivalry between the New York Yankees and Boston Red Sox in the years after World War II. Halberstam's work can be supplemented with two books by the talented sports journalist Peter Golenbock: *Dynasty: The New York Yankees, 1949–1964* (Englewood Cliffs, N.J., 1975) and *Fenway: An Unexpurgated History of the Boston Red Sox* (New York, 1992). Golenbock also wrote one of the definitive studies of the Dodgers, *Bums—An Oral History of the Brooklyn Dodgers* (New York, 1984). For the Dodgers there is also the highly effective if overly sentimental study by Roger Kahn, *The Boys of Summer* (New York, 1972)

The franchise shifts that transformed baseball in the 1950s have produced excellent analyses. Kuklick's *To Every Thing a Season* discusses the problems that plagued the Athletics. For the Dodgers and Giants the best source is Neil Sullivan, *The Dodgers Move West* (New York, 1987). Sullivan shows the complexity of the reasons for the move of the Giants and Dodgers to California, avoiding the Walter O'Malley-as-villain analysis that can be found in many books about baseball in the 1950s. For the creation of a new Baltimore franchise, James Miller, *The Baseball Business: Pursuing Pennants and Profits in Baltimore* (Chapel Hill, 1990) is a solid scholarly treatment that focuses on the reasons baseball succeeded in Baltimore.

The clash between management and labor from the 1960s on, revolving around free agency and the ending of the reserve clause, is dealt with by Lee Lowenfish, *The Imperfect Diamond: A History of Baseball's Labor Wars* (New York, 1980. For the growing militancy of the players' union, see Marvin Miller, *A Whole Different Ball Game: The Sport and Business of Baseball* (New York, 1991). Management's problems are highlighted in Bowie Kuhn, *Hardball* (Lincoln, Nebr., 1989). Kuhn's autobiography is graphic proof that he would have made a good commissioner after World War II but was out of his depth in the labor conflicts of the 1970s. John

Helyar, *Lords of the Realm: The Real History of Baseball* (New York, 1994) focuses on the obtuseness of the baseball owners.

The growing economic problems of baseball in the 1970s and 1980s are discussed in a number of sources. The best are Ken M. Jennings, *Balls and Strikes: The Money Game in Professional Baseball* (New York, 1990); Jesse Markham and Paul Teplitz, *Baseball Economics and Public Policy* (Lexington, Mass., 1981); and Gerald W. Scully, *The Business of Major League Baseball* (Chicago, 1989). These studies show the complexities of the economic challenges facing baseball over the last two generations since the ending of the reserve clause and the emergence of free agency. They also help to explain the shift of power to the players and away from the owners who had run baseball since its origin as a professional sport.

Roger Noll, ed., *Government and the Sports Business* (Washington, D.C., 1974) and James Quirk and Rodney D. Fort, *Pay Dirt: The Business of Professional Team Sports* (Princeton, 1992) place the economic issues facing baseball in the broader context of the emergence of big-time sports in America.

Anyone doing research on baseball's past will find certain publications invaluable. The *Sporting News*, once known as "the Bible of Baseball," is a grand source for the history of the game. Until the early 1970s it concentrated almost exclusively on baseball. It can be supplemented—especially over the past thirty years—with the yearly publication, the *Sporting News Baseball Guide*, a compendium of the events of the preceding season.

Finally no one can study baseball without turning to one of the great sports publications of recent history, *The Baseball Encyclopedia* published by Macmillan. I used the ninth edition published in 1993. First appearing in 1969, *The Baseball Encyclopedia* quickly became a necessity for any serious student of baseball. It contains the record of anyone who ever played professional baseball, a summary of every season, records of every baseball trade, and a list of various baseball statistical achievements by year and for a career. It is quite simply indispensable.

# Index

Aaron, Hank, 157, 161, 175
Abernathy, Ted, 179
Adams, Franklin P., 70
Adelman, Melvin, viii
Alcohol abuse in baseball, 36–37, 66–67
Alexander, Grover Cleveland, 80, 92, 116, 137
All-Star Game, 134–136
Allen, Richie, 187
Alou, Felipe, 165
Alou, Matty, 175
Alston, Walter, 214
American Association, 29, 30, 31, 41, 42, 46, 51–52
American Baseball Guild, 152
American Broadcasting Co. (ABC), 170
American Protective Society, 35
Amherst College, 13
Anaheim Angels, 171
Anderson, Dave, 207
Anderson, George "Sparky," 214
*Angels in the Outfield*, 212
Anson, Adrian "Cap," 26, 32, 34, 35, 42
Aparicio, Luis, 165, 183
Arledge, Roone, 173
Arroyo, Luis, 179
Atlantic City Bacharach Giants, 111
Attell, Abe, 102

Attendance figures, 75, 82, 87–88, 92, 97–98, 103, 123, 143–144, 158–159, 170, 172, 196, 207–208
Autry, Gene, 171

Bagwell, Jeff, 206
Baker Bowl, 41, 123–124
Baker, Frank "Home Run," 71, 81, 82, 88
Baker, Newton D., 93
Baker, William, 123–124
Ball, Philip de Catesby, 84, 89, 126
Baltimore Orioles, 55–56, 161, 182
Bando, Sal, 182, 189
*Bang the Drum Slowly*, 3
Banks, Ernie, 157
Barber, Walter "Red," 127, 132, 139
Barnes, Ross, 26
Barrow, Ed, 100, 114, 129
Barry, Jack, 81, 88
Baseball Players Fraternity, 86
Basketball, professional, 174
Baylor, Elgin, 174
*Beadle's Dime Base-Ball Player*, 8
Beazley, Johnny, 132
Beery, Wallace, 39
Bench, Johnny, 202
Bender, Albert "Chief," 70–71, 81, 86, 88
Berra, Lawrence "Yogi," viii, 198
Bierbauer, Lewis, 51
Black Sox scandal, 66–67, 103–106

Blackmun, Harry, 187
Boggs, Wade, 202
Bonilla, Bobby, 195
Boston Beaneaters, 53, 55–56
Boston Braves, 92, 160
Boston Pilgrims, 67–68, 76
Boston Red Sox, 91–93, 99–100, 103, 125, 150
Boston Red Stockings, 18–21, 32
Breadon, Sam, 132
Bresnahan, Roger, 80
Brett, George, 202
Brock, Lou, 157, 183
Brooklyn Bridegrooms, 43
Brooklyn Dodgers, 131–132, 149–150, 158, 162–163
Brooklyn Eckfords, 11, 19
Brooklyn Robins, 91
Brooklyn Superbas, 58
Brouthers, Dan, 37
Brown, Mordecai "Three Finger," 70, 86
Brown, Tommy, 142
Browning, Pete, 36
Brush, John T., 45, 58, 68–69
Bryant, Bear, 173
Bulkeley, Morgan, 27, 137
Burke, Mike, 176

California Angels, 171
Camp, Walter, 58
Campanella, Roy, 156
Campaneris, Bert, 189
Campbell, Bill, 189
Cannon, Robert, 184
Carlton, Steve, 198, 202
Carpenter, Robert, 124
Carter, Gary, 195, 202
Carter, Jimmy, 192
Cartwright, Alexander, 7–8, 136, 137
"Casey at the Bat," 38–39
Casey, Dan, 39
Casey, Hugh, 179
Cash, Dave, 189
Castro, Fidel, 175
Cepeda, Orlando, 165, 175
Chadwick, Henry, 8–9, 10, 20, 28, 40, 138
Chalmers award, 133

Chamberlain, Wilt, 174
Chance, Frank, 101
Chandler, A. B. "Happy," 151
Chase, Hal, 109
Chicago Cubs, 70–71, 77, 93
Chicago Tribune Co., 198
Chicago White Sox, 70, 78, 92, 98, 165
Chicago White Stockings, 19, 38
Christopher, George, 163
Cicotte, Eddie, 101–102, 105, 108
Cincinnati Red Stockings, 15–17, 20, 26
Cincinnati Reds, 98, 100–102, 126–127
Civil War, 11–13, 110
Clark Foundation, 135–137
Clarke, Fred, 67
Clarkson, John, 37
Cleland, Alexander, 136
Clemente, Roberto, 165, 175, 216
Cleveland Forest Citys, 19
Cleveland Indians, 149, 155, 159
Cleveland Spiders, 55
Clift, Harlond, 126
Clinton, Bill, 206
Cobb, Ty, vii, 56, 71, 80, 87, 93, 101, 105, 137, 183
Coca-Cola, 185
Cochrane, Mickey, 117, 124
Collins, Eddie, 71, 81, 88, 100, 125
Collins, Jimmy, 56, 63
Colorado Rockies, 197
Columbia Broadcasting System (CBS), 181–182
Comiskey, Charles, 61–62, 78, 99, 101–102, 106, 125
Comiskey Park, 78–79
Connor, Roger, 37, 44
Continental League, 170
Coombs, Earle, 114
Coombs, Jack, 71
Cooper, Mort, 132
Cooper, Walker, 131
Coors, Joseph, 197
Cramer, Roger "Doc," 125
Crawford, "Wahoo" Sam, 80
Cricket, 4–6, 15, 22
Cronin, Joe, 125

Crosetti, Frank, 129
Crosley Field, 127
Crosley, Powel, 126–127
Crusinberry, Jim, 102
Cy Young award, 134, 199

Day, John, 46
Dean, Jerome "Dizzy," 131
Dean, Paul, 131
Delehanty, Ed, 63–64, 66–67
Dempsey, Jack, 109
Derringer, Paul, 127
Designated hitter (DH) rule,
    180–181
Detroit Tigers, 56, 71, 98, 143, 182
Detroit Wolverines, 42
Devore, Josh, 82
Dickey, Bill, 129, 130
DiMaggio, Joe, 129, 131, 142,
    148–149, 182, 185, 214
Dineen, Bill, 68
Disney, Walt, 39
Doby, Larry, 156
Doerr, Bobby, 125
Doubleday, Abner, 3, 14, 136, 137
Dreyfuss, Barney, 66, 68, 78, 99, 125
Drysdale, Don, 184
Duffy, Hugh, 56
Durocher, Leo, 132, 214
Dykes, Jimmy, 117
Dykstra, Lenny, 195

Ebbets, Charles, 90
Ebbets Field, 76, 132, 163
Eckersley, Dennis, 199
Eckert, William, 186
Edison, Thomas Alva, 39
Eisenhower, Dwight D., 169
Eller, Hod, 101
Estella, Roberto, 150
Etten, Nick, 143
Ewing, Buck, 37, 44
Ewing, George, 4

Federal League, 83–91
Feller, Bob, 142, 155, 178
Fenway Park, 77
Fernandez, Chico, 166
*Field of Dreams,* 212

Fingers, Rollie, 182
Finley, Charles O., 182, 188, 193
Fisk, Carlton, 202
Flick, Elmer, 63–64
Flood, Curt, 187–188
Florida Marlins, 197
Foley, Tony, 21
Football, college, 58, 173
Football, professional, 173–174
Forbes Field, 78–79
Ford, Whitey, 178, 181
Fort Wayne Kekiongas, 19
Foster, George, 195
Foster, Rube, 35, 109–111
Foxx, Jimmie, 117, 124, 206
Frazee, Harry, 99, 103, 155
Free agency, 187–189
Freedman, Stephen, viii
Freeman, Andrew, 59, 62
Frick, Ford, 137
Frisch, Frankie, 113, 116, 153, 214
Fullerton, Hugh, 102
Fultz, Dave, 86, 91–92

Gambling, 60, 66–67. *See also* Black
    Sox scandal.
Gandil, Chick, 101, 108
Gardella, Danny, 150
Garland, Wayne, 189
Gehrig, Lou, 104, 114, 122, 129–130,
    155, 182
Giamatti, Bart, 203–204
Gibson, Bob, 157, 176, 178, 215
Gilmore, James, 84–85, 88–90
Glassop, Jack, 31
Gleason, Kid, 100
Gomez, Lefty, 129
Gonzalez, Tony, 165
Gooden, Dwight, 195
Goodman, Ival, 127
Gordon, Joe, 130, 149
Gossage, Goose, 129
Gowdy, Hank, 92
Grant, Charles "Tokohoma," 110
Grant, Frank, 34, 100
Green Bay Packers, 173–174
Greenberg, Hank, 142, 214
Griffey, Ken, 205, 215
Griffith, Clark, 61, 63, 125, 143

Groh, Heinie, 101
Grove, Lefty, 117, 124
Gulick, Luther, 57
Gullet, Don, 189
Gwynn, Tony, 202, 205

Haas, Walter, 197
Hafey, Chick, 116
Haines, Jess, 116
Hall of Fame, 136–138
Hamilton, "Sliding" Billy, 56
Haney, Fred, 171
Hanlon, Ned, 21, 58
*Harper's Weekly,* 16–17
Harridge, Will, 135, 148
Harriman, Averell, 164
Harris, Mark, 3
Hatfield, Jim, 20
Hayes, Woody, 173
Hearst, William Randolph, 38
Henrich, Tommy, 130, 149
Hernandez, Keith, 195
Hernandez, Willie, 200
Herrmann, Garry, 66, 99
Heydler, John, 56, 180
Higgins, Pinky, 125
Hilldale Baseball club, 111
Hiller, John, 179
Hodges, Gil, 156
Hooper, Harry, 71
Hoover, Herbert, 121
Hopper, De Wolf, 38
Hornsby, Rogers, 104, 116, 128
Houston Astros, 170
Houston Colt 45s, 170
Howard, Elston, 181
Huggins, Miller, 114, 128
Huizenga, Wayne, 197
Hulbert, William, 26–28, 31
Hunter, Jim "Catfish," 182

Irabu, Hideki, 216
Irvin, Monte, 156–157, 176
Isaminger, James, 165

Jackson, Reggie, 157, 182, 215
Jackson, "Shoeless" Joe, 80, 100, 105, 108
Jacoby, Brook, 201

James, Bill, 57
Jennings, Hughie, 55–56
Johnson, Al, 45
Johnson, Arnold, 162
Johnson, Byron "Ban," 59, 60–63, 65–66, 92, 99, 106, 213
Johnson, Hiram, 106
Johnson, Tom "Golden," 45
Johnson, Walter, 70, 81, 87, 137

Kaat, Jim, 178
Kansas City Monarchs, 155
Kansas City Royals, 196
Kauff, Benny, 89, 92
Keefe, Tim, 34, 37–39, 44
Keeler, "Wee Willie," 55
Keller, Charley "King Kong," 130, 149
Kelly, George "Highpockets," 113
Kelly, Mike "King," 32–36, 40, 213
Kennedy, John F., 169
Kinder, Ellis, 179
Kiner, Ralph, 82
Klein, Chuck, 105
Koppett, Leonard, 201
Koufax, Sandy, 177–178, 184
Krause, Harry, 81
Kubek, Tony, 181
Kuhn, Bowie, 186, 193, 196, 203

Lajoie, Napoleon, 63–64, 137
Lakefront Stadium (Chicago), 41
Landis, Kenesaw Mountain, 66, 105–109, 123, 126, 130, 135, 138, 141–142
Lanier, Max, 132, 151
Lardner, Ring, 3
Lasker, Albert, 106
Lazzeri, Tony, 116, 129
Leach, Tommy, 67
League of Colored Base Ball Clubs, 35
Lincoln, Abraham, 13
Lisenbee, Hod, 142
Lloyd, John Henry, 110
Lombardi, Ernie, 127
Lombardi, Vince, 173
Los Angeles Angels, 171
Los Angeles Dodgers, 163–165

Los Angeles Lakers, 174
Louis, Joe, 214
Lowden, Frank, 107
Lowe, Bobby, 56
Lyle, Sparky, 199

Mack, Connie, 21, 56, 61–64, 69–71,
    81–82, 101, 113, 116–117, 124,
    135, 137, 162, 214
Mack, Earle, 162
Mack, Roy, 162
MacPhail, Larry, 126–127, 132,
    139–140, 154
Maglie, Sal, 152
Maharg, Billy, 105
Major league franchises, cost of, 77,
    197
Major League Baseball Players
    Association, 153, 184
Malamud, Bernard, 3
Mantle, Mickey, 156, 174, 181–182
Maranville, Walter "Rabbit," 87
Marichal, Juan, 165, 175, 178
Marion, Marty, 131, 151
Maris, Roger, 181, 207, 216
Martin, Fred, 151
Martin, Pepper, 131
Massachusetts game, 7
Mathews, Eddie, 161
Mathewson, Christy, 70, 81, 93, 113,
    137
Mauch, Gene, 214
Mays, Carl, 99
Mays, Willie, 156–157, 174, 215
McAdoo, William Gibbs, 106
McAlpin, Edwin, 45
McCarthy, Joe, 128–130, 214
McCormick, Frank, 127
McDowell, Sam, 178
McGinnis, Stuffy, 81
McGinnity, Joe "Iron Man," 70,
    113
McGraw, Frank "Tug," 199
McGraw, John, 21, 55, 66, 68–69,
    81–82, 92, 101, 113, 135, 137,
    214
McGreevy, "Nuf Ced," 76
McGwire, Mark, 207–208
McKnight, Denny, 29–31

McLain, Denny, 177–178
McNally, Dave, 188
McQuinn, George, 126
Merkle, Fred, 82
Messersmith, Andy, 188
Meusel, Bob, 114
Meusel, Emil "Irish," 104, 113
Mexican League, 90, 113
Meyers, "Chief," 82
Miller, Bing, 117
Miller, Marvin, 183–189, 193–194,
    203–207
Mills, A. G., 31
Milwaukee Braves, 161
Minoso, Minnie, 165
Miracle Braves, 88
Mize, Johnny, 131, 148
Monaghan, Tom, 197
Monday Night Football, 173
Montreal Expos, 171
Montreal Royals, 155
Moore, Terry, 132
Moran, Pat, 100
Morgan, Cy, 81
Morgan, Joe, 215
Moses, Robert, 163–164
Most Valuable Player award,
    133–134
Mullane, "Handsome" Tony, 31
Municipal Stadium (Cleveland), 159
Murphy Money, 153
Murphy, Robert, 152–153
Musial, Stan, 131–132, 148, 151, 180

Namath, Joe, 174
National Agreement, 31–32, 41,
    61–62, 99
National Association of Base Ball
    Players, 14–15, 18–19
National Association of Professional
    Base Ball Players, 19, 26
National Brotherhood of Base Ball,
    44–45, 47–48
National Commission, 65, 85
*Natural, The,* 3
Negro Leagues, 109–112
New Frontier, 169
*New York Clipper,* 40
New York game, 7–8

New York Giants, 38, 42, 55, 65, 81–82, 92, 98, 158
New York Knickerbockers, 7, 15
New York Mets, 170–171, 195
New York Mutuals, 13, 18–20
New York Yankees, 98, 128–131, 150, 158, 181, 207
Newcombe, Don, 156
Newhouser, Hal, 151, 178
Nichols, Charles "Kid," 56
Nicholson, Bill, 143
Niekro, Phil, 202
Night baseball, 140–141
Nixon, Richard M., 191
Nomo, Hideo, 21
*No, No, Nanette,* 191
Noll, Roger, 206
Norworth, Jack, 76
Nugent, Gerry, 124

Oakland Athletics, 182
O'Doul, Lefty, 124
Oliva, Tony, 175
Olmo, Luis, 150
O'Malley, Walter, 162–164, 171
Orosco, Jesse, 200
Ott, Mel, 105
Owen, Mickey, 151
Owens, Jesse, 176

Page, Joe, 179
Pagliarulo, Mike, 201
Paige, Leroy "Satchel," 156
Palmer, A. Mitchell, 97
Pascual, Camillo, 166, 175
Pasquel brothers, 150
Perini, Lou, 160–161
Peters, Hank, 194
Philadelphia Athletics, 19–20, 65, 69–70, 87–88, 116–117, 161–162
Philadelphia game, 6
Philadelphia Phillies, 57, 63, 79, 91, 123–124
Pigeon, Frank, 11
Pittsburgh Pirates, 68, 78, 165
Plank, Eddie, 71, 81, 86, 88
Players League, 47, 63
Pollet, Howie, 131–132
Polo Grounds, 41, 104, 114

Poulson, Nelson, 163
Protective Association of Professional Base Ball Players, 62, 86
Pulitzer, Joseph, 25
Pulliam, Harry, 65–66

Quinn, John, 160

Radbourne, Charles "Old Hoss," 37–38
Radio broadcasting of baseball, 138–140
Ramos, Pedro, 166
Ravitch, Richard, 205
Reach, A. J., 40–41
*Reach's Guide,* 40, 47, 83
Red Scare, 97, 105
Reese, Pee Wee, 156
Relief pitching, 179–180, 198, 200
Repoz, Roger, 182
Reserve clause, 30–33, 43, 64, 65, 152, 185, 187–189
Reyes, Nap, 150
Reynolds, Allie, 149
Richards, Paul, 161
Rickey, Branch, 115–116, 125, 131–132, 150, 154–156, 159, 216
Rigney, Bill, 171
Rizzuto, Phil, 130, 149
Robinson, Frank, 157
Robinson, Jackie, viii, 149, 154–156, 176, 215
Robinson, Wilbert, 91
Rockefeller, John D., 107
Rockford Forest Citys, 19
Rogers, John, 46, 63–64
Rolfe, Red, 129
Roosevelt, Franklin D., 140–142
Roosevelt, Theodore, 107, 169
Rose, Pete, 204
Rothstein, Arnold, 102
Roush, Edd, 100–101
Rozelle Rule, 193
Rudi, Joe, 189
Ruether, Dutch, 101
Ruffing, Red, 129
Ruppert, Jacob, 99, 103, 113–114, 125, 128

Russell, Bill, 174
Ruth, George Herman "Babe," viii, 82, 91, 103–105, 118, 122, 128, 137, 155, 180, 206
Ryan, Nolan, 202

Sallee, Slim, 101
Samuel, Juan, 195
San Francisco Giants, 164, 165
Sandberg, Ryne, 193
Schoendienst, "Red," 155
Seattle Mariners, 196–197
Seaver, Tom, 202
Seitz, Peter, 188
Selig, Bud, 204, 206
Seymour, Harold, vii
Shawkey, Bob, 128
Sheets, Larry, 201
Sherman Anti-Trust Act, 64, 90, 107
Shibe, Ben, 62, 77
Shibe, Tom, 62
Shibe Park, 76–78, 79, 124, 159
Short, Bob, 187
Simmons, Al, 117, 124, 214
Sinclair, Harry, 84, 90
Sisler, George, 99, 104, 126, 137
Slaughter, Enos "Country," 131–132
Smith, Lee, 199
Smith, Ozzie, 202
Snider, Duke, 156
Soden, Arthur, 32
Somers, Charles, 62
Sosa, Sammy, 207–208, 216
Soto, Mario, 198
Sotomayer, Sonia, 207
Southworth, Billy, 132
Spahn, Warren, 161
Spalding, Albert Goodwill, 9, 21–22, 26, 44, 46, 58, 67, 135
*Spalding's Official Base Ball Guide,* 40
Speaker, Tris, 71, 80, 91, 100, 137
Spink brothers, 40
*Sporting Life,* 40, 46
*Sporting News,* 40, 46, 102, 134
*Sports Illustrated,* 40
Steinbrenner, George, 16
Stern, Bill, 13

Stirnweiss, George "Snuffy," 143
Stengel, Casey, viii, 171, 214
St. Louis Browns, 42, 99, 125–126, 143, 160
St. Louis Cardinals, 89, 115, 131
Stoneham, Charles, 77
Stoneham, Horace, 164
Stovey, George, 34
Stovey, Harry, 51
Strawberry, Darryl, 195
Strikes in baseball: 1981, 194–195; 1994, 203–207
Sullivan, John L., 34–35, 213
Super Bowl, 174
Sutton, Don, 202
Sweeney, Charles, 31, 36

Taft, William Howard, 79, 83, 106
"Take Me Out to the Ball-Game," 76
Tammany Hall, 20
Taylor, Tony, 166
Teapot Dome scandal, 84
Tebeau, Pat, 57
Tekulve, Kent, 199
Television and baseball, 159
Temple Cup, 55
Temple, William, 54
Tener, John, 100
Thayer, Ernest Lawrence, 39
Thayer, Frank, 11
Thigpen, Bobby, 199
Thompson, Sam, 37
Thrall, A. E., 54
Tiant, Luis, 177
Tinker, Joe, 70, 86
"Tinker to Evers to Chance," 70
Topping, Dan, 181
Topps Chewing Gum Co., 185
Torre, Joe, 207
Town ball, 4
Troy Haymakers, 19
Twain, Mark, 26
Tweed, William Marcy, 20
Tygiel, Jules, viii

Ueberroth, Peter, 196, 203
Union League, 30, 41
Usery, William, 207

Veeck, Bill, 156, 161, 186
Versalles, Zoilo, 175
Vincent, Fay, 204
Voigt, David, vii, 43
Von der Ahe, Chris, 36, 52

Waddell, Rube, 70–71
Wagner, Honus, 67, 71, 91, 137, 153, 202
Wagner, Robert, 164
Walker, Moses Fleetwood, 35
Walker, Tilly, 100, 105
Walters, Bucky, 127
Ward, Arch, 134
Ward brothers, 84, 88
Ward, John Montgomery, 34, 40, 44–45, 47
Washington Nationals, 19
Washington Olympics, 19
Washington Senators, 65, 87, 125, 166
Watergate, 191
Weaver, Buck, 108
Weaver, Earl, 200
Webb, Del, 181
Weeghman, Charles, 89
Weiss, George, 130
Welch, Mickey, 36
White, Deacon, 26
White, Sol, 34

Wilkinson, J. L., 111
Williams, Cy, 104–105
Williams, Ken, 105
Williams, Lefty, 100, 102
Williams, Matt, 205
Williams, Ted, 108, 125, 142, 160, 185
Williamson, Ned, 100
Willis, Vic, 56
Wills, Maury, 157, 183
Wilson, Hack, 105, 118
Wilson, Woodrow, 80, 83, 97
World Series, 67–68, 70–71, 80–82, 88, 92–93, 100–103, 129, 158, 199
Wright, George, 15
Wright, Harry, 15, 18, 21–22
Wrigley Field, 77
Wrigley, Philip K., 164
Wrigley, William, 128

Yankee Stadium, 114–115
Yastrzemski, Carl, 180
Yawkey, Tom, 125, 127
"You Know Me Al," 3
Young, Cy, 63, 68
Young, Dick, 186
Young, Nick, 59
Yount, Robin, 202

## A NOTE ON THE AUTHOR

John Rossi was born and grew up in Philadelphia, and studied at La Salle College, the University of Notre Dame, and the University of Pennsylvania, where he received a Ph.D. in history. His chief interests, on which he has written widely, are British politics and American baseball. His books include *The Transformation of the British Liberal Party* and *A Whole New Game: Off the Field Changes in Baseball, 1946–1960*. Mr. Rossi is now professor of history at La Salle University in Philadelphia.